Epistemology

the theory of knowledge

philosophy
in focus

Daniel Cardinal
Jeremy Hayward
Gerald Jones

Academic consultant
Stephen Law

JOHN MURRAY

Authors

Daniel Cardinal is Head of Philosophy at Orpington College and teaches Philosophy at Birkbeck Faculty of Continuing Education; **Jeremy Hayward** is a lecturer at the Institute of Education, London, where he is the subject leader for the PGCE in Citizenship education; **Gerald Jones** is Head of Humanities at the Mary Ward Centre, London.

The academic consultant **Stephen Law** is a lecturer in Philosophy at Heythrop College, University of London, author of *The Philosophy Files*, the popular introduction to Philosophy, and editor of the journal *Think*, published by the Royal Institute of Philosophy.

The cover image shows a detail from *The Incredulity of St Thomas* by Michelangelo Merisi da Caravaggio (1571–1610), courtesy of Schloss Sanssouci, Potsdam, Germany/Bridgeman Art Library/Alinari. To see the full picture, visit: www.kfki.hu/~arthp/html/c/caravagg/06/34thomas.html
Although every effort was made to ensure that the above website address was correct at the time of going to press, John Murray (Publishers) Ltd cannot be held responsible for its contents.

A scheme of work is available from the publishers. Please call 020 7873 6000 and ask for Educational Marketing.

© Daniel Cardinal, Jeremy Hayward and Gerald Jones 2004

First published in 2004
by Hodder Murray, a member of the Hodder Headline Group
338 Euston Road
London NW1 3BH

Reprinted 2004, 2005, 2006

Artwork by Tony Jones/Art Construction, Tony Randell
Cover design by John Townson/Creation

Typeset in 11/13pt Galliard by Dorchester Typesetting, Dorchester, Dorset
Printed and bound in Malta

A CIP catalogue record for this book is available from the British Library.

ISBN-10: 0 7195 7967 8
ISBN-13: 978 0 719 57967 7

Contents

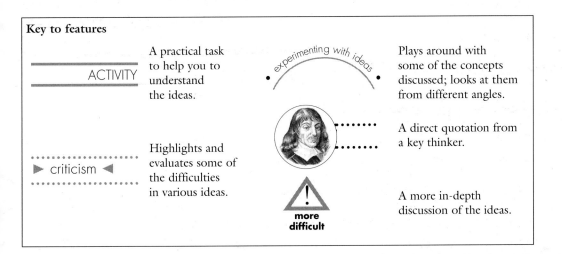

Key to features

ACTIVITY

A practical task to help you to understand the ideas.

experimenting with ideas

Plays around with some of the concepts discussed; looks at them from different angles.

A direct quotation from a key thinker.

► criticism ◄

Highlights and evaluates some of the difficulties in various ideas.

! more difficult

A more in-depth discussion of the ideas.

The series

This series is aimed at students who are beginning to study philosophy. The books fill the 'middle ground' between introductory texts, which do not always provide enough detail to help students with their essays and examinations, and more advanced academic texts, which are often too complex for new philosophy students to understand.

All of the study guides are written around the themes and texts for the AQA AS level philosophy specification. In addition to *Epistemology: The Theory of Knowledge* there are five more to be published:

- Plato's *Republic*
- Descartes' *Meditations*
- Sartre's *Existentialism and Humanism*
- *Philosophy of Religion*
- *Moral Philosophy.*

The authors are writers with substantial experience of teaching philosophy at A level. They are also committed to making philosophy as accessible and engaging as possible, and so the study guides contain exercises to help students to grasp the philosophical theories and ideas that they will face.

Feedback and comments on these study guides would be welcome.

Words in SMALL CAPITALS are explained in the Glossary on pages 145–50.

Introduction

From the dawn of civilisation humans have tried to make sense of the world around them. In their efforts to explain, understand and, ultimately, to control their world, they have produced a bewildering variety of systems of thought and practice, from mythologies, religions and philosophies, to mathematics and scientific theories. One important function of these systems is to provide humans with beliefs about the true nature of reality. But how accurate are these beliefs? Do any of them amount to genuine knowledge about the world? It may be that the human mind can never fathom the depths of reality so that there are aspects of the universe that must remain forever mysterious.

Such considerations are enormous in their scope. They deal with the relationship between the human mind and the universe, and as such they concern everything we think and do. But such broad and abstract questions are also amongst the most difficult to answer. Our species' ongoing attempt to grapple with such questions forms the subject we now call the *theory of* KNOWLEDGE or EPISTEMOLOGY, a term derived from the Ancient Greek words *episteme* meaning 'knowledge' and *logos* meaning 'account', or 'rationale'.

Epistemology is often seen as the central field of enquiry in modern philosophy. However, because epistemology discusses the nature of knowledge and belief itself, its concerns reach far beyond the confines of philosophy and touch on every area of modern thought and study. Every academic discipline throws up questions of method, validity and truth: in other words, epistemological questions. But epistemology is not just of academic concern. One distinctive feature of human beings is the extent of their capacity to pass on the knowledge they acquire to future generations. Before the advent of the written word, this would be done by demonstrating skills to others or through oral instruction. The invention of writing, about 3000 BC, made it possible to pass a far greater amount of knowledge from one generation to the next. At the same time, knowledge so recorded can be transported readily across great distances. In short, writing allows for knowledge to be stored independently of the minds of human beings and this has had a profound effect on the way we live. Some commentators suggest that the internet, and the speed with which it distributes information, places us on the brink of another knowledge revolution. To get a sense of how important the communication of knowledge is, imagine the world today with no means of recording and sharing knowledge. How would we cope? What would become of the world in a matter of one or two generations?

In our individual lives, knowledge also holds a core position. My system of BELIEFS effectively determines all my actions. For example, it is only because I believe that tomorrow I will be hungry, along with various other beliefs I have about the whereabouts of shops, transport options and so on, that I can decide to go out grocery shopping today and succeed in my plan. Without true beliefs the basic practicalities of life would be impossible. On a more sophisticated level, my political, moral and religious beliefs determine how I treat other people, which way I vote, my attitude to life and death and so on. My network of beliefs defines the kind of person I am.

So how do philosophers go about producing a *theory* of knowledge? Indeed, what exactly is knowledge in the first place? Is it just one thing, or many different things? Is it a kind of thing at all? These are some of the questions we'll be looking at in this book. One thing to note about them straight away is that the answers to them are far from obvious. Indeed, it is not obvious what the answers would look like, nor how we should even begin to think about finding them! This uncomfortable situation is typical in philosophy. Part of what makes philosophical questions so puzzling is that we don't know the best way to go about answering them and this can make it very difficult even to get started.

However, rather than get all het up at this stage about the right way to theorise about knowledge, it is probably best just to get on with doing it. A good way to start is to reflect on the things that we know and believe, in order to understand their importance. The short thinking exercise or 'thought experiment' below is designed to do this.

experimenting with ideas

Imagine a time capsule that could be sent back in time 2000 years, to Ancient Rome. Unfortunately, the time capsule is rather small and can hold only half a side of A4 paper. What would you write on the paper that would change the world for the better? What knowledge would you send back in time? Suppose that what you write will be translated into Latin and that the Romans will take it seriously.

1 Create the half side of A4 that you would send back in time. Remember that the Romans will have no extra help in understanding what is written, so you will have to explain everything in terms they understand.

2 Outline how you think the knowledge on your piece of paper would change the world.

3 Lastly, consider what this exercise reveals about the nature of knowledge.

Feedback on part 3 of the task

What does this exercise tell us about the nature of knowledge? Here are some possible answers. Note that these are only suggestions, and there are many other important things to say about knowledge that you may have turned up. Some of these are discussed next when we consider the 'fundamental concepts in epistemology'.

- There are many *different kinds of knowledge*. Some can be communicated in words; others in diagrams or maps. However some kinds of knowledge, such as how to tie your shoelaces or perform the kiss of life, are very difficult to express in language or to draw. They can best be communicated by actually showing someone.

- You may have found that people in the past would appreciate having some new pieces of knowledge. Why? Well, the simple answer is that *knowledge can be very useful.* Knowing things helps us to achieve what we want. The great discoveries of the past have had a huge impact on our lives.

- You may have found it difficult to write down what you know in a useful way. So why might this be? Some of the difficulty may be due to a further point to note about knowledge – namely, that each item of knowledge assumes knowledge of many other things, so it is difficult to express on its own. Everything we know is connected to lots of other things we know and believe. This is especially true of things we know now that are most useful to us. So, for a culture 2000 years ago with a very different set of beliefs, new but disconnected pieces of knowledge would not be of much use. What this suggests is that *the value of knowledge is in part to do with the system of beliefs into which it fits.*

- You may have been tempted to put moral maxims on the sheet of paper – such as, 'it is wrong to keep slaves', or 'treat all humans equally'. This shows that *it is not just knowledge of facts that are important in shaping the world*, but also our moral beliefs.

- The exercise also may have shown how very few of us now have any useful scientific knowledge. Yet we live in a society that depends upon such knowledge. This shows how much, *as a society, we collect and pool our knowledge* and specialist abilities. Each of us knows only a little of what society as a whole does.

3

■ You may also have been unsure of whether you know something or not; or how you can be sure you know something. This raises an important difficulty, namely how to establish that we really do know. One way of trying to show that we know is to find EVIDENCE for our knowledge. So it seems that *knowledge needs support by evidence*.

The structure of the book

Having had an initial opportunity to think broadly about the importance of knowledge and beliefs, we can now introduce the main questions we will be exploring in this book. Epistemology is a vast field, both in scope and in the variety of different approaches to the subject that philosophers have taken. Consequently, no book of this size can tackle all of the issues. We have chosen to focus on a cluster of concepts that are central to many of the key debates in epistemology. Note, however, that the themes and issues dealt with in one chapter overlap considerably with those in the other chapters.

■ Chapter 2: Knowledge and justification

As we have seen above, knowledge is very important, and on a personal level our beliefs affect everything we do. But we don't want to hold any old beliefs; it is crucially important that we acquire the right ones, as FALSE beliefs can be extremely dangerous. A false belief about what sort of mushrooms are edible could cost you your life. Similarly, a false belief that humans can fly by jumping from tall buildings whilst vigorously flapping their arms could lead to clear difficulties. So ideally we want to avoid holding false beliefs and make efforts to ensure our beliefs are true. But how is this to be done?

In most cases we will have some sort of *evidence* or *justification* that leads us to hold a belief. For example, you might believe something to be true because someone told it to you in the pub, you saw it on the news, or you read it in a book. Generally, the better this evidence is, the more justified we feel in holding the belief. But how can we be certain that the evidence on which we base our belief is reliable? We could always produce further evidence to prove the truth of the initial evidence. But again, why do we think this further evidence is true? Are we going to need evidence to justify our evidence to justify our evidence? If so, where will our search for justification end? This raises the question of whether any of our beliefs are justified ultimately. In this chapter we will examine such questions and explore ways of defending our ordinary beliefs against an extreme sceptic who claims we cannot achieve knowledge about anything.

Chapter 3: Rationalism, empiricism and the structure of knowledge

What are the main sources of knowledge? A historically significant dispute within philosophy hinges on whether the primary source of human knowledge is *experience* or REASON. Those philosophers who argue that our knowledge is founded in experience gathered through the five senses are called *empiricists*. Those who argue that we acquire our most important knowledge through the application of reason are called *rationalists*. In this chapter we will explore some of the major arguments attacking and defending these two positions. Traditionally, both rationalists and empiricists have been agreed on one point, namely that knowledge is structured like a building, with basic or foundational beliefs at the bottom, supporting or justifying an edifice of further beliefs. In this chapter we examine this view and some difficulties with it, as well as presenting two further accounts of the structure of knowledge: COHERENTISM and RELIABILISM.

Chapter 4: Knowledge and perception

Another central question within modern philosophy has been how we acquire knowledge of the world around us. It seems natural to say that our senses reveal the world to us as it really is, but a small amount of philosophy throws doubt on this idea. For example, objects, as they move away from me, *appear* smaller but I know that they do not actually get smaller. So the world cannot be exactly as it appears. Once we start to make a distinction between the world as it appears to us and the world as it really is, then the problem arises of how we can tell which features are real and which are mere appearances. For example, are objects really coloured? Or are colours just the way things appear to us when certain wavelengths of light enter our eyes? Does a tree that falls unheard in a forest actually make a noise, or is a noise something that by definition has to be experienced by a mind? Perhaps the world is very different from how it appears. In fact, can we really be sure that the world exists at all? These, and other issues related to perceptual knowledge, are considered in Chapter 4.

Chapter 5: The concept of knowledge

A final, yet equally central, concern of epistemology has been to determine what precisely we mean by 'knowledge' or by saying we 'know'. In other words, philosophers have tried to provide an analysis of the *concept* of knowledge. Traditionally it has been claimed that to say that I *know* is to say that I have a *belief* which is *true* and for which I have reasonable evidence which justifies my holding the belief. In this chapter we will explore the merits of this attempt to understand the concept of knowledge.

To start thinking about some of these topics, complete the questionnaire below. Remember that there are no right or wrong answers since the point is to explore the nature of your own beliefs and knowledge claims. It's probably best not to think too deeply about your responses, but to opt for the response that immediately occurs to you as the best, or that your common sense would suggest is closest. When you have completed the questionnaire, read the introduction to Chapter 2: Knowledge and justification, and consider the questions on page 8.

Questionnaire: what you know and what you believe

Read through the following statements. For each of them decide whether or not:

a) you know it
b) you don't know it
c) you believe it, or
d) you don't believe it.

1 There is life elsewhere in the universe.

2 Absence makes the heart grow fonder.

3 Your hand is in front of you now.

4 Colours exist in the world.

5 Shakespeare wrote *Hamlet*.

6 2 + 2 = 4

7 Miracles happen.

8 The world is round.

9 If you drop a coin it will fall downwards.

10 The sun will come up tomorrow.

11 You are not dreaming at the moment.

12 John F. Kennedy was killed by a lone gunman.

13 Siberia exists and is very cold in winter.

14 Men have landed on the moon.

15 Other people have inner experiences like you.

16 There is a spiritual dimension to the universe.

17 A bird in the hand is worth two in the bush.

18 Science can't explain everything.

19 God exists.

20 Most of your beliefs are true.

Knowledge and justification

Introduction

In everyday life we reckon we know all kinds of things. For example, if you are reading this book, you probably know how to tie your shoelaces, what an apple tastes like, how old you are, and what you get if you add three to five. So much seems fairly obvious. But philosophers are concerned to ask what it is that enables us to know such things as these. How can we tell when we really know something, rather than just thinking we do? What justifies us in claiming to actually know something? To begin thinking about these questions, consider how you would respond if a friend were to come up to you and tell you that Tony Blair was in fact a woman. After your initial surprise, you would doubtless respond by saying something like: 'I don't believe you!' or 'How do you know that?' In other words, you would be sceptical about your friend's claim, and would ask her to offer some evidence or JUSTIFICATION for it. In response, your friend might well attempt some form of justification. For example, she might say one of the following:

- 'I read it in the *Sunday Sport*.'
- 'A friend told me, and he's studying politics at college.'
- 'I saw a very detailed photograph on the internet.'

Once again, consider how you would respond to your friend at this point. Probably, you would not be persuaded that Tony Blair was a woman. But why not? A plausible initial answer is that none of these three responses represents a good enough justification for your friend's claim. They are just not strong enough reasons for believing it. But what would count as a good justification in this instance?

One answer might be that you had medically examined Tony Blair and discovered her to be a woman, or had performed surgery on him and turned him into one. In these cases, the direct evidence of your own experience would appear to be a good justification for a belief. What other kinds of evidence can you think of that would justify this belief? The following exercise explores the idea of justification.

1 Revisit the questionnaire on page 6. Ask yourself *why* you believe or know these things. What is it that leads you to believe it? In other words, think about the *justification* you have for your claim. Take note of one justification for each claim.

2 Classify your justifications into different types. See if you can isolate a few basic ways in which a belief can be justified. (One way to do this is to ask what the *source* of your knowledge or belief is. For example, did you see it for yourself? Or did you hear about it from someone else, such as from a teacher or a book? Is it just common knowledge?)

3 Is it possible to cast doubt on any of the justifications? Think about how you could do this. Which kind of justification do you think is the strongest? Are there any things you know with 100 per cent certainty? Think of the strengths and weaknesses of each type of justification. Consider what life would be like if you couldn't acquire knowledge in each of these ways.

4 Lastly, consider how you distinguished the elements you claimed to *know* from those you claimed merely to *believe*. In other words, what makes the claims to knowledge different from the others? Do they all have something in common? On the basis of this, could you come up with a definition of 'knowledge'?

Feedback on part 1 of the task

An important point to note about both knowledge and belief is that we don't generally claim to know or believe something for no reason. We normally regard it as unsatisfactory if we ask how someone knows something or why they believe something and they say that they 'just do'. The feeling here is that there must be some basis that inclines you to believe something rather than its opposite.

Feedback on part 2 of the task

What different sorts of justification did you find? To explore different possible answers, let's begin with the example of the belief that feathers fall more slowly than cannonballs. What might have led you to this belief? Here are some possible answers.

■ *Common knowledge*
It can appear that some beliefs are simply part of common knowledge, part of the fund of beliefs that everyone holds. So you might think that everyone knows that cannonballs fall quicker than feathers. Despite this, if we look more closely at this belief, it seems that we can find a further origin or basis for it, and so find that it is justified in one of the following ways.

- *Personal experience*
  You may have watched feathers and cannonballs falling off windowsills and so seen for yourself. If so, you would be justifying your belief by appealing to your own personal experience.
- *Testimony of others*
  Alternatively, someone may have told you – a scientist perhaps – that cannonballs fall faster than feathers. So you would have learned it from another person's testimony. This category would include information gained from reading or from television.
- *Justified by other beliefs*
  Suppose you happen to hold the following two beliefs:

  a) that heavier things fall more quickly than lighter things;
  b) that cannonballs are heavier than feathers.

  You could then work out that cannonballs fall faster than feathers. Here you would have used reason and other beliefs to arrive at this new belief. So your belief would be justified by appealing to other beliefs.
- *Worked out by thinking*
  Another category of justification you may have found concerns beliefs you can work out just by thinking about them. For example, we can work out the answers to sums by thought alone, or, as philosophers have it, by the use of reason. With a little thought, we can work out that 8 added to 13 makes 21. So, it seems, knowledge of maths can be justified by the use of reason. (However, the belief that feathers fall more slowly than cannonballs is not something we could work out in this way. We can't acquire this belief simply by thinking about feathers and cannonballs.) We'll be looking more at this kind of knowledge in Chapter 3, and asking what kinds of belief we can and cannot justify in this way.

Feedback on part 3 of the task

Note that each of the above ways of justifying a belief can be questioned. For example, common sense is often wrong. It would once have been common sense to suppose that the Earth is flat, but this has turned out not to be true. Also, our own experience is not always reliable. We can make mistakes. It may be that what we thought was a cannonball was in fact a black balloon filled with air. Similarly, we can't always trust the testimony of other people. They too can be mistaken, or may want to deceive us. Also, the reliability of appealing to other beliefs depends on their being true. Is it really true that lighter things always fall more slowly than heavier things? Well, in fact it is not. On the moon, for example, where there is no air resistance, all objects fall at the same speed and acceleration irrespective of their weight. While it may be very difficult to imagine being mistaken about simple sums, all of us make mistakes and so reason is not foolproof either. None the less, some ways of justifying beliefs appear more reliable than others, so what are the advantages and disadvantages of the justifications we've isolated here?

- *Common sense*
  One important advantage of common sense is its usefulness. Common-sense assumptions about the world enable us to get on with our lives. Someone who has no common sense has a difficult time performing the most basic tasks. A disadvantage, however, is that common knowledge need not always be true. Just because many people assume something is the case, doesn't mean they are right.

- *Personal experience*
  Knowledge acquired by personal experience seems more direct and certain. While secondhand knowledge may sometimes lead us astray, it is very difficult to doubt something that we've experienced for ourselves. On the other hand, beliefs acquired this way are comparatively limited in scope. There is very little we can learn directly on our own.

- *Testimony of others*
  Knowledge acquired from others has the advantage of increasing the stock of knowledge we have as individuals. Indeed, we acquire most of what we claim to know in this way. However, this increase in scope comes at a price – beliefs acquired from others are less certain. Because they are acquired indirectly there is more room for doubt about them.

- *Justified by other beliefs*
  By reasoning on the basis of beliefs we already hold, we can again extend their range and number. But we can't learn anything totally new in this way, since the scope will ultimately be limited to what is implicit in the things already known. So to acquire new knowledge we need to return to personal experience or to others' testimony.

- *Worked out by thinking*
  While it is very hard to doubt the basic judgements of mathematics, again an important disadvantage of this form of justification is that the truths we can work out in this way are very limited. Knowing about maths is all very well, but it can tell us little new information about the world around us.

These considerations suggest that there may be a pay-off between the *certainty* of our beliefs and their *extent*. In other words, the more we can count as knowledge, the less certain it is. The more demanding our account of what counts as knowledge, the less things we can know.

We've seen that beliefs need to be justified if we are to have reason to hold them. We've also seen that there are different kinds of justification, some of which may be stronger than others. In this chapter we will be exploring the different ways in which we justify our beliefs to try to find out what makes for a good justification and what makes for a bad one. In particular, we will be concerned with the question: Is there any way of justifying a belief that leaves no room for doubt whatsoever? In other words, can we find a complete justification for our beliefs?

The chapter is divided as follows:

- Justifying our beliefs
- Philosophical scepticism and the problem of justification
- Defeating the sceptic
- Ways of defeating the sceptic
- Conclusion
- Key points you need to know about knowledge and justification.

Justifying our beliefs

Appealing to other beliefs

We've seen that one way we justify our beliefs is by appealing to further beliefs that we hold. To give another example, my belief that my cat – Casanova – is hungry is based on various other things I believe about him: that he hasn't eaten for two days, that he has a big appetite, that he won't stop pestering me with mournful miaows, and so on. Or I may justify the belief that Madonna is the greatest female solo artist of all time by appealing to various other beliefs I have concerning the way she transforms her image year on year, her never-ending stream of catchy top ten hits, the failure of her peers from the 1980s and 1990s to maintain an audience, and so on. What is involved here is an INFERENCE from one set of beliefs to another, where an inference is the move that we make when we reason from one or more claims to a conclusion.

It is an important aspect of any justification that the further evidence we appeal to must be relevant, and must also be worthy of belief. If I am trying to justify my belief in Madonna's artistic genius it is no good my appealing to further beliefs which have nothing to recommend them.

So a justification that appealed to her brilliant career as a film star would be no good whatsoever if her films have been consistently awful. A justification of a claim to knowledge is only as good as the evidence supporting it. In other words, the evidence I appeal to needs to be true if it is to count as proper evidence.

This is perhaps obvious. But unfortunately this can very quickly lead us into difficulty. Before exploring this difficulty, consider the following dialogue:

> **Laura:** *Here's an amazing fact. Did you know that the Amazon crocodile cannot stick its tongue out?*
> **Luke:** *I don't believe it! How do you know?*
> **Laura:** *I saw it on 'Nature Watch' on the telly.*
> **Luke:** *How can you possibly regard 'Nature Watch' as a reliable source of information? It could be that it is in the pay of Brazilian coffee producers who have a vested interest in spreading disinformation about crocodiles.*
> **Laura:** *Ah, I thought you might say that, so I've cross-checked with a reputable encyclopedia, which stated quite clearly that Amazon crocodiles cannot stick their tongues out.*
> **Luke:** *But that evidence is also unreliable. It may be that this myth about crocodiles has been around for some time and all the experts have been taken in. So it could be that the vast majority of reputable encyclopedias carry this error.*
> **Laura:** *Well, actually I have been to South America and checked for myself. I examined several crocodiles along the Amazon and none of them could stick their tongues out.*
> **Luke:** *Ah, but it's always possible that the coffee producers saw you coming and somehow engineered it so that you would only encounter crocodiles without tongues.*

There are several things to note about this dialogue. What strikes people immediately is the silliness of Luke's doubts. Luke appears interested in being sceptical simply in order to irritate Laura. Moreover, he has no good evidence for supposing that there is an elaborate conspiracy among coffee producers. His sceptical scenarios are increasingly unlikely as the dialogue progresses and so his argument is not one we would be inclined to take seriously.

While all this is true, it misses the philosophical points that the dialogue is intended to illustrate. SCEPTICISM in philosophy is a peculiar thing and not at all like scepticism in ordinary life. Luke is indeed being rather silly, and philosophers can appear silly too. So, before we can see the more serious point lying behind Luke's scepticism, let's briefly outline the nature and purpose of philosophical scepticism.

Philosophical scepticism and the problem of justification

Philosophical scepticism and ordinary scepticism

There are three important points to note about philosophical scepticism:

1 Philosophical scepticism is used to test the strength of our knowledge claims. The sceptic asks questions of the evidence supporting the knowledge claims we hold, and if we cannot provide adequate answers, the sceptic demands that we give up the claims. At the same time, if we can refute the sceptic, we will have vindicated our claim to know. So, by trying to defeat sceptical arguments, philosophers hope to clarify what we can and cannot know and to establish the certainty with which we can claim knowledge. Also, through dialogue with scepticism, epistemologists hope to come to a better understanding of the nature of knowledge and justification.

2 Scepticism in philosophy differs from scepticism in ordinary life. One such difference concerns the kinds of things that are doubted. In ordinary life we might well doubt whether a train will arrive on time, whether aliens exist, or whether a monarchy is a good system of government. But philosophers go one step further. Philosophers tend to doubt things that in ordinary life are very difficult, if not impossible, to doubt. For example, they may question whether or not their own hand really exists, whether other people could really be zombies with no thoughts or feelings whatsoever, or whether we can know that the sun will rise tomorrow. By attempting to doubt assumptions such as these, epistemologists hope to come to an understanding of what underlies our most basic beliefs concerning physical objects, other people and the future.

3 Another important difference is that in ordinary life we tend to doubt something only when we think it could well be false. However, when philosophers doubt something they may actually believe it to be true. So while a philosopher may doubt the existence of the physical objects that she sees around her for the sake of argument, this does not imply that she really thinks they don't exist. Rather, her doubt implies that she wants to establish whether the reasons we have for thinking they exist are good ones, and so her doubts will normally have no impact on how she behaves. The philosopher will continue to lean on the very table she pretends to doubt exists, and will continue talking

to you even while she doubts that you have a mind. This is one reason why philosophical doubt often appears silly. The philosopher's doubts appear pointless since they can have no bearing on the practicalities of life. They also seem far-fetched, and even insane. But their doubts don't arise because philosophers suffer from paranoid delusions. Rather, philosophical doubt is a theoretical exercise designed to discover what we can know.

The infinite regress of justification

With this in mind, it becomes clear that the force of Luke's scepticism in the dialogue above does not rely on his scenarios being likely or believable, but only on whether they are remotely possible, and as yet unrefuted. If they are even a remote possibility, then Laura's claims to know are in some way undermined. Luke, instead of being an irritating cynic, may well be interested in seeing whether any of our justifications are completely foolproof.

The real interest of the dialogue concerns its *structure* and the general sceptical point that this structure reveals. Laura has to appeal to evidence – to further beliefs – in order to support her claims to know. But the beliefs she appeals to must themselves count as known if they are to play an adequate supporting role. As we have seen, if I justify a belief by appeal to a further belief, then this further belief must itself be worthy of assent. This seems to mean that this further belief will have to be known. But if Laura needs to have knowledge of her evidence then she will need to be able to justify that evidence in turn by appeal to further evidence. This means that the process of producing evidence to justify one's beliefs can have no end. Thus any claim to knowledge is caught in a vicious infinite regress, which makes us question whether any of our beliefs are justified at all. The inevitable sceptical conclusion appears to follow: *we cannot know anything.*

The infinite regress argument suggests that, in the final analysis, none of our beliefs is justified. The whole of our belief system rests on nothing. It's as if we've suddenly discovered that the ground had been pulled from under us and that we no longer have reason to believe anything at all. This is a serious problem not only for philosophers interested in understanding how we justify our beliefs but also, it would seem, for anyone who holds any beliefs at all!

■ Figure 2.1 *The infinite regress of justification*

For a belief to be known it must be supported by a good reason, and the reason will be something else we believe. This second belief must also be supported by some further reason. This leads to an infinite regress, and it seems that there can be nothing to give any ultimate support to our knowledge claims. So the sceptic concludes that nothing can be known.

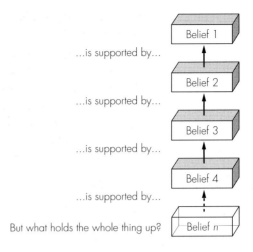

...is supported by...

...is supported by...

...is supported by...

...is supported by...

But what holds the whole thing up?

Every sceptical argument presents us with a dilemma: we must either accept its conclusion or reject it. If we accept it, we will have to try to fit it in with the rest of our beliefs in such a way that we can be comfortable with it. If we reject it, we must find something wrong with the argument that leads to it. Accepting the sceptic's conclusion that justification is ultimately impossible puts us in a difficult position. If all justifications are unfounded, then it seems as though we have no good reason to believe one thing rather than another. If any justification is as groundless as any other we might as well flip a coin to decide what we should believe. Clearly, if this argument is sound it threatens to undermine our whole belief system. Is it possible for us to resist the sceptical argument and so avoid this conclusion?

Stopping the infinite regress

There are different possible reactions to the problem posed by infinite regress of justification. One response, which you may have thought of, is to search for special 'regress-ending' beliefs that could be known to be true without evidence or supporting reasons. Such beliefs could be known without the need for further justification, perhaps because they are able to justify themselves. If such beliefs could be found, then the regress could be stopped and we would have a firm basis on which to establish our knowledge claims. The beliefs that justify themselves or need no justification we can call *foundational* beliefs, since they are the basic ones on top of which all others are built, or in terms of which all the others are justified. This is the classical reaction to the regress argument, and any theory of knowledge and justification that is committed to the existence of such foundational beliefs is termed FOUNDATIONALISM.

Philosophical scepticism exercise

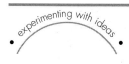

experimenting with ideas

Below are five typical examples of sceptical arguments. Each makes us question the nature of our beliefs about the world, and casts doubt on our claims to knowledge. A sceptical argument presents us with a dilemma. Either we reject the conclusion, in which case we must find something wrong with the argument, or we accept the conclusion, in which case we have to try to fit it in with the rest of our belief system.

1 Read through each argument. Then ask yourself whether you find the sceptical conclusion (**in bold**) acceptable.

    a) If you reject the conclusion, then try to think of ways in which the conclusion might be avoided. Where does the argument go wrong? Does it make any erroneous assumptions? Is there something wrong with the reasoning process? Note your thoughts.

    b) If you accept the conclusion, try to explain why the conclusion is not as unpalatable as it first appears. What impact does the sceptical conclusion have on your belief system as a whole? Does the conclusion require you to give up much of what you usually take for granted? Is it compatible with a considered understanding of what we can and cannot know? Note your thoughts.

1 Infinite regress of reasons

Suppose someone claims to know that the Amazon is the longest river in the world. How can you be sure she knows? The obvious way is to ask her what evidence she has for her belief. Perhaps she was told so by a competent and honest geographer or read it in an encyclopedia. But then how does she know that the geographer hasn't made a rare mistake, or that the encyclopedia hasn't misprinted the length of the Amazon? Again, supporting reasons need to be provided. She might cross-check against maps, other encyclopedias and geographers, and so forth. But the sceptic could point out that the original measurement on which all these records are based could have been mistaken. So perhaps to be sure that she knew she would have to travel to South America and measure the river for herself. But again, the sceptic could ask how she could know that her measuring equipment is accurate. This process of sceptical questioning would appear to have no end. So any claim to knowledge is caught in a vicious infinite regress and so knowledge about the physical world is impossible.

This example argues that if I claim to know something, then I must be able to justify it by appeal to evidence, since otherwise I am simply making an unsubstantiated claim.

Moreover, a claim to knowledge is only as good as the evidence supporting it. So it would appear that I need to be sure of my evidence and consequently need to have knowledge of that, too. But if I need to have knowledge of my evidence then I will need to be able to justify that evidence in turn by appeal to further evidence. Since the process of justification has no end, the sceptic's conclusion is that **we cannot acquire knowledge**.

2 Closed belief system[1]

Imagine you have a friend who begins to develop paranoid delusions. He believes that the government is watching him and plans to do away with him because of what he knows about alien plans to take over the world. He is convinced that his phone is bugged, the newspapers have secret coded messages about him, and that people are following him wherever he goes. You try to convince him that none of this is true. For example, you open up the phone to reveal that there are no bugs. Your friend, however, responds that they must have special methods to hide them in the wires, or perhaps MI5 have people working undercover for the phone company. You point out that the people he thinks are following him are different people each time. But he responds that this is because they are all masters of disguise. Whatever you say or do he remains unconvinced. He even begins to suspect that you are saying all this because you're in on the conspiracy.

Imagine further that your friend is a member of a strange cult, which is convinced that aliens are taking over the world. Members of the cult have all kinds of weird evidence to support their belief. If you try to point out that such evidence is silly, they argue that you are too brainwashed to recognise it. If you point to contrary evidence, they reject this as being part of the government cover-up. Nothing you say or do will sway them from their belief.

The belief system of your friend and of his cult seems immune from revision and yet they are obviously crazy. But isn't your system of beliefs equally immune from revision? Aren't you also in the grip of a self-sustaining set of beliefs? If so, how can you be sure that your belief system is not equally crazy? Maybe the cult is right and it is you who is brainwashed! Perhaps most of your beliefs are as baseless as those of your friend. If this is possible, then the sceptic argues that all your beliefs might be part of a closed belief system that is false, so **you don't know anything**.

■ 3 Descartes' dreaming argument (from *Meditation I*[2])

On occasion you dream that you are engaged in the normal activities of everyday life. For example, you may dream that you wake up, have a shower, eat breakfast, and so on. You may even dream that you travel to college, go to a philosophy class and ponder deep problems; or are reading about scepticism, much as you are now. While having such a dream there is nothing within the dream that you could point to which would show that it was a dream and not waking life. Everything in the dream happens just as it does when you are awake. Since the experience within such dreams is indistinguishable from waking life, you cannot be sure that you are not dreaming now. But if it is possible that you are currently dreaming, then you cannot be sure that any of the things you are experiencing are real. It follows, therefore, that **you do not know that this room or any of the people and things in it exists**.

■ 4 Brain in a vat (cf. Descartes' 'evil demon' argument, *Meditation I*[3])

Imagine this science-fiction story.

The year is 2560. Scientists know an enormous amount about the workings of the human brain to the point where they are able to keep brains alive, suspended in a vat of chemicals and nutrients. One fiendishly clever (yet slightly mad) scientist is working on a pet project of his own. He has acquired one such brain, which he plays with in his secret laboratory. The scientist has carefully wired up the brain's input and output nerves to a powerful computer. The computer is able to send a complex array of electrical impulses which mimic precisely those that a normal brain-in-a-body would receive from its environment through its senses. The computer interacts with the brain in such a way as to maintain an illusion that the brain is in fact a complete human being with arms and legs, living a normal life. Further, the brain is fooled into believing that it is living in the early part of the twenty-first century and that it has been alive in this period all of its 'life'. The brain is fooled into believing that it has friends, eats food, speaks English, and so on, and that right at this very moment it is reading a strange science-fiction story in a book on epistemology.

In fact, this is not a science-fiction story. The story is true, and you are that brain. You have been deceived about every single aspect of your entire life. The year is really 2560 and everything you thought you knew about yourself and the world is false. Is this plausible? Is it a remote possibility? However remote, if it is indeed a possibility then **you cannot know that anything you think is real actually exists, or that anything you've done has actually happened.**

5 Scepticism about knowledge of the future (cf. Hume's Enquiry Concerning Human Understanding[4])

In our ordinary lives there are certain things about the world that we take for granted. For example, I expect the sun to rise in the morning, objects to fall when dropped, the neighbour's dog to bark as I leave my house and not suddenly to start speaking Chinese, and so forth. But what evidence do we have for these beliefs? Why do we suppose we know that dogs won't suddenly start to speak to us in Chinese, or that gravity won't suddenly work in reverse?

The obvious answer is that gravity has always worked that way, and dogs have never spoken Chinese, and so we have no reason to think that such things will change now. But is this a good response? Notice that it presupposes that the future resembles the past, since it is saying that dogs will continue to behave as they always have and that objects will fall down just as before. But why should we suppose that the future will resemble the past? Maybe tomorrow things will be very different. After all, think of a poor turkey fed grain for 364 days, who wakes up on Christmas morning expecting the same again, only this time it is to be tragically disappointed. In blindly assuming that the future must resemble the past we may end up as disappointed as this turkey.

In response to this, we might accept that it is *possible* that things will change, but none the less insist that, generally speaking, the past is a good indicator of what the future will hold. After all, this supposition has worked well so far, so it's sensible to stick with it. Unfortunately, the fact that (generally speaking) the future has resembled the past *in the past* goes no way to establishing the claim that it will continue to do so *in the future*. To think it does is once again to use evidence from the past to make claims about the future, and this move is the very thing being questioned. So our general belief that past experience is a reliable guide to the future cannot be justified, since any appeal to past experience inevitably begs the question, or presupposes what it is trying to prove. In other words, it amounts to saying that the future resembles the past because the future resembles the past and argues in a circle. **Therefore we cannot gain knowledge of the future.**

From this exercise on philosophical scepticism we have seen the variety of weapons the sceptic has at her disposal to undermine our claims to know. Some arguments claim that our beliefs cannot be *certain*, others that our *justification* or *evidence* is inadequate, others that our beliefs cannot be shown to be *true*. This suggests that certainty, justification, evidence and truth are important elements of what we normally think of as knowledge. If we don't have these, the sceptic says, then we cannot have knowledge. We may want to question whether knowledge really does involve any of these elements, and this question will be dealt with in detail in Chapter 5 when we try to work out precisely what knowledge is.

Before we do, however, it is worth examining briefly the relationship of certainty to knowledge since it is important not to confuse the two. Some people are inclined to think that to know something truly you must be absolutely certain of it. After all, it may seem that you can't really know something so long as you harbour doubts. Others may be less strict, concerned that if we have to be absolutely certain, then we may end up with very little that we can really know. Although in the past philosophers have tended to value certainty very highly, most philosophers these days do not think you need to be certain of something to know it, as we will see in Chapter 5.[5] It is worth remembering this as sceptical arguments can have a tendency to make us search for certainty as a way of overcoming them. The idea here is that beliefs that are absolutely certain can never be undermined. Having resisted the sceptic in this way, the tendency can then be to take the further step of supposing that in order to know something you must be absolutely certain of it, and that you can't really be said to know if you aren't certain. But while this is a possible position, it is important to be aware that it is not the only one.

1 Consider whether you hold any beliefs which cannot be doubted. In other words, are there things you know which are not susceptible to the sceptical arguments above? Such beliefs are often termed INDUBITABLE.

2 Once you have come up with some indubitable beliefs, consider what is distinctive about them. What makes them different from the kinds of belief that do succumb to scepticism?

3 Lastly, consider why confirming knowledge to indubitable beliefs might be very limiting.

Defeating the sceptic

René Descartes (1596–1650) is the most famous philosopher directly to take on the task of defeating scepticism. Descartes was born in France and educated at a Jesuit college. Thereafter he travelled in Europe extensively, for some of this time as an officer in the army. When he was a young man, he had strange and vivid dreams on consecutive nights, which would shape his life. His dreams told him that it was his mission to seek the truth using reason – and this he spent the rest of his life doing. As well as being famous for his philosophical writings, Descartes is an important figure in mathematics. Many students will keenly remember plotting lines and shapes on X–Y axes, in other words using Cartesian co-ordinates which Descartes invented (Cartesian means 'of Descartes'). Throughout his life Descartes was fond of lying in bed of a morning 'thinking'. In his later life he was persuaded to move to Sweden to teach Queen Christina. The Queen required her philosophy lessons to begin at five in the morning. Descartes died after about six months of this new regime.

Following his mission to seek the truth through reason, Descartes examined many of his beliefs. He noticed that the beliefs he had held from an early age had turned out to be false, and that his ordinary belief system appeared to be full of errors and contained little of which he could be certain. He felt he needed to start again and see if he could build a system of beliefs that was completely certain. The best way to do this, he decided, would be to tackle scepticism head on. If he could defeat it, then he would have good reason to claim to have knowledge. So he used a method that began by employing the most radical sceptical arguments he could muster. This method – the so-called METHOD OF DOUBT – tried to suspend judgement about *all* the things he previously took for granted. Everything that could possibly be doubted was treated as false for the purposes of argument. So the very possibility of doubt about something was, for Descartes, sufficient for treating it as false. If, after following this method, he arrived at something which could not be doubted, i.e. something which was *indubitable*, then he would have reached a point of absolute certainty. At that point, he hoped, he might start to rebuild a new system of beliefs, which would be free from errors.

You can read about Descartes' attempt to defeat the sceptic and build a new system of knowledge based on certainty in his book, the *Meditations on First Philosophy*. In the first of the six *Meditations*, Descartes begins by noting that his senses have sometimes deceived him. For example, he has, from time to time, been the victim of illusions. In accordance with his method of doubt, he therefore resolves not to trust his senses any more, for 'it is prudent never to trust entirely those who have once deceived us'.[6] Descartes considers the objection that this is a rather extreme reaction to the fact of the occasional illusion. Surely, only a mad person wouldn't trust his senses? But, continues Descartes, are we not equally deluded as a mad person when we dream? When dreaming we often believe ourselves to be people, and to be in places which we are not. And how can I be sure that I am not dreaming now? If this could be a dream, then I cannot be sure that anything appearing around me is real. None the less, Descartes reckons, whether or not I am dreaming it remains the case that the things I am dreaming about must have some basis in reality. So is there anything in my dream that must have existence? Perhaps I can only be sure that shapes and colours are real. It is at this point that Descartes introduces his most radical sceptical scenario.

The evil demon

Descartes

I shall suppose, therefore, that there is, not a true God, who is the sovereign source of truth, but some evil demon, no less cunning and deceiving than powerful, who has used all his artifice to deceive me. I will suppose that the heavens, the air, the earth, colours, shapes, sounds and all external things that we see, are only illusions and deceptions which he uses to take me in.[7]

A powerful demon such as this could make anything appear to be the case. Your whole life could be a fiction created by the demon. In reality you may not even be a human being. You could be anything: a marmot, a mushroom, or something else that you have never even heard of; and this EVIL DEMON is simply creating sensations in your mind to make it look as if you are a human living on a planet called Earth, reading of these bizarre possibilities. It's important to realise that Descartes is not saying that he thinks it likely that there is such a demon bent on deceiving us. His argument rests only on its being a conceivable possibility. If it is possible, he is saying, then we can't know for sure that it is not true. And if we can't know it's not true, we can't know anything which depends on its not being true.

Descartes came up with the idea of a deceiving demon nearly 400 years ago, yet the central insight is evident in some modern science fiction scenarios such as *The Matrix*. We could be being deceived by some extremely sophisticated machine, or by our brains being kept in a vat and fed false sensory information (see point 4 on page 18). The point is still the same. Can you be 100 per cent sure that you are not being deceived in this way? If you concede that this is a possibility, however absurd or remote, then surely you can never be 100 per cent certain of anything again. Perhaps nothing can be known. Perhaps you don't even exist at all. At this point, Descartes produces a response that is probably the best known philosophical argument of all.

Descartes

No indeed; I existed without a doubt, by the fact that I was persuaded or indeed by the mere fact that I thought at all.[8]

My own existence cannot be doubted because, when I attempt to doubt it, I recognise that there must be something doing the doubting, and that something is me. So at the time of thinking Descartes cannot be nothing. His own existence can be known for certain in the face of his most radical doubts. Here Descartes discovers the first principle, the first certainty that he has been searching for. It is often termed the COGITO, after the Latin formulation from his *Principles of Philosophy* (1644), namely: *cogito ergo sum*, meaning 'I am thinking therefore I exist', or 'I think therefore I am'.

Descartes

While we thus reject all that of which we can possibly doubt, and feign that it is false, it is easy to suppose that there is no God, nor heaven, nor bodies, and that we possess neither hands, nor feet, nor indeed any body; but we cannot in the same way conceive that we who doubt these things are not; for there is a contradiction in conceiving that what thinks does not at the same time as it thinks, exist. And hence this conclusion, I think, therefore I am, is the first and most certain of all that occurs to one who philosophises in an orderly way.[9]

The *cogito*

Descartes was looking for a way of defeating the sceptic, for something that could not be doubted, and it looks as if he found it. It is impossible to doubt your own existence, for the very fact that you are doubting implies that you exist. What is so significant about the *cogito* is that it can be known to be true just by thinking it. Here, my conviction in my own existence appears unshakable. It doesn't depend for its truth upon anything else, and so appears to justify itself. This is

23

precisely what we were looking for: a self-justifying belief from which to rebuild a body of knowledge. But has Descartes really defeated the sceptic? And, if so, what exactly has he established?

Focusing on the latter question, Descartes is claiming to have established that '*I am, I exist*'.[10] But what exactly is this I? Descartes realises that he has not yet established the existence of himself as a human being, for the evil demon could still be deceiving him as to his earthly form. He may not even have a body. But he claims that the *I* must be something, and that at the very least it must be a thing that can think – a thinking thing, or, in other words, a conscious being. He feels sure that no demon could deceive him in this.

But is this so? Some commentators feel that Descartes has only established the existence of some thoughts or conscious experiences. Can Descartes assert that these experiences belong to any self or *I*? Perhaps thoughts can exist by themselves, not owned by any thinker? If thoughts can exist on their own, then Descartes is over-reaching in claiming 'I am'.[11]

Although criticisms are possible, many would agree that Descartes has shown us a way to stop the slide into scepticism. But perhaps the *cogito* is not the only way. Maybe scepticism is not as powerful as it first appears and we can find further ways of resisting its advance.

Ways of defeating the sceptic

Transcendental arguments

more difficult

The *cogito* is one of the most scrutinised philosophical arguments of all time. One of the big concerns has been to determine what sort of ARGUMENT it is. How exactly does it work as an argument? Although there is no universal agreement (there rarely is in philosophy), many argue that the important point is that it defeats doubt about one's own existence by showing that it is impossible to doubt if one doesn't exist. In other words, existence is a necessary condition for doubt to occur, and so the very act of doubting actually proves one's existence. The attempt to doubt one's own existence is, in other words, self-defeating. Arguments that have this sort of structure are termed TRANSCENDENTAL arguments (a term first used in this way by the great German philosopher Immanuel Kant, 1724–1804). Such arguments ask what the conditions of possibility are for something being the case. Here, my own existence is a condition of possibility for my doubt. Perhaps one's existence is not the only thing that defeats doubt in this way. What other things must be the case for doubt to exist? To consider this, look at this activity.

Ways of defeating the sceptic

ACTIVITY   Below is a list of beliefs that you probably hold.

1 Go through each in turn and try doubting it.
2 What difficulties are encountered in attempting to doubt them? Note any difficulties that occur to you.

a) Language exists.
b) You are aware of having experiences.
c) You hold beliefs that can be true or false.
d) You can doubt various things.
e) Your reasoning ability is reliable.
f) Knowledge is possible.

Activity feedback
Here are some possible answers. Note that there are numerous other possible answers you may have found, but those here all have something in common. Can you put your finger on what it is? Do you think this defeats the sceptic?

a) Language exists. *If you were seriously to doubt that language existed, how would you express or formulate your doubts? Presumably they could only really be formulated in language. You would have to think or say something like, 'I doubt language exists'. But in the act of formulating your doubts you are using language, the very thing you are supposed to be doubting. So such a doubt would appear to defeat itself as soon as it was expressed.*

b) You are aware of having experiences. *Focus on a particular experience you are having and try to doubt that you are having it. For example, if you are seeing a white page before you with dark letters printed on it, try to doubt that you are having this experience. It would seem impossible to do. It is certainly possible to doubt that the page and the writing actually exist. Perhaps you are hallucinating. But it seems impossible to doubt you are having the experience of the page. Whether this experience is caused by a demon, hallucinogens or even reality, you are still having the experience. It's as though in the very act of having an experience, you are directly aware that you are having it, and can't doubt that you are having it.*

c) You hold beliefs that can be true or false. *To doubt that you hold beliefs is to believe that it is possible that you don't have any beliefs. But this is itself a belief. So if you believe this you have at least one belief, and so you cannot consistently doubt that you hold beliefs.*

d) You can doubt various things. *To doubt that you can doubt things involves doubting. So you can't consistently doubt that you can doubt.*

e) Your reasoning ability is reliable. *If you doubt the reliability of your own reasoning abilities then you won't be able to make any progress in any argument whatsoever. Any piece of reasoning is suspect. This would mean that you would have to doubt the validity of the arguments that led you to doubt your reason in the first place.*

f) Knowledge is possible. *If you deny that knowledge is possible, then you can't know anything, including the claim that knowledge is not possible.*

Global scepticism

Recall that Descartes began his enterprise by raising doubts about *all* his previous beliefs. To doubt all your beliefs is to claim a *global* or universal scepticism. It is often argued that such global scepticism is not as easy as Descartes made it appear. So what difficulties does it face?

First, it is important to note that to claim to doubt *all* beliefs quickly leads into problems. To consistently doubt *all* beliefs involves doubting the very statement of global scepticism itself. To claim that 'all beliefs are doubtful' implies that the very belief 'all beliefs are doubtful' is itself doubtful. Thus global scepticism cannot be stated coherently without also bringing itself into question. To put the problem another way, consider the claim that 'nothing can be known'. Either this claim can be known or it can't. So can it be known? If it can then there is one claim that can be known, namely that 'nothing can be known', and so the claim is false and it can't be known. Therefore it can't be known that 'nothing can be known'. This is an important discovery made by the Ancient Greeks. It shows that not everything can be doubted at once, and if we are to doubt one set of beliefs we are also going to have to take certain other beliefs for granted.

Doubting our senses completely

Now let's reconsider the argument for illusion, as used to cast doubt upon the senses. Can this argument be resisted too? The sceptic points out that our senses sometimes deceive us, and draws the conclusion that they could always be deceiving us. So the argument can be summarised as follows:

■ *Our senses sometimes deceive us.*
Therefore perhaps they always deceive us.

But consider another argument of similar form:

> ■ *Some paintings are forgeries.*
> *Therefore perhaps all paintings are forgeries.*

It is clear that there is something wrong with the second argument. From the fact that paintings are sometimes forgeries, it does not follow that they all could be. Indeed, the conclusion is actually inconsistent with the premise that they sometimes are. Since a forgery is a copy of a genuine (non-forged) painting, the existence of the former actually requires the existence of the latter. You can't have a forgery if you don't have original paintings. And you wouldn't know that there were forgeries unless you were able, at least sometimes, to identify a painting as an original.

So what of the first argument? If the two arguments are analogous then there must be something wrong with it too. From the fact that we are sometimes deceived it would not follow that we might always be. This seems to be right, for the way in which we discover that our senses have, in fact, deceived us is by contrasting the deception with a genuine PERCEPTION in the same way that we distinguish forged from original paintings. We notice that the senses sometimes deceive, precisely because we can identify and correct errors.

To understand this point, imagine I look in the distance and see what I take to be a bus, but which upon walking closer turns out to be only a pillar-box. In the first case I was deceived, but I only become aware that I was deceived because I assume that in the second case I genuinely see what is there: a pillar-box. So the fact that we are aware that sense deception takes place from time to time actually presupposes that for the rest of the time our senses do not deceive us.[12] This suggests that the method of doubt cannot be pushed so far as to undermine *all* beliefs about what our senses reveal to us, since to do so we would have to abandon various beliefs upon which the sceptical argument is premised. So we can only deploy the concept of doubt meaningfully against a background of general certainty.

In this connection consider also how the sceptic may appeal to science in order subsequently to throw doubt on the truthfulness – or *veracity* – of what we claim to know through perception. The sceptic may argue that we cannot have *knowledge* of what we perceive, because what we perceive is very different from what science tells us is really out there. For example, science tells us that physical objects don't have smooth surfaces as they appear to, but are composed of tiny atoms and in fact consist mostly of empty space. However, in this example, the sceptic is taking one area of knowledge, namely that matter is composed of atoms, to cast doubt upon another, the veracity of our perception. The argument trades on scientific knowledge in a way that is self-defeating, for it relies on claims about the composition of matter, which could only be known if we could trust our senses. Scientific knowledge itself, after all, is acquired through perception. The conclusion must be that no universal scepticism about perception can rely on an argument of this sort.

Is Descartes' doubt genuine?

Consider Descartes' efforts to doubt the senses and consider the possibility that the physical world doesn't exist. Is this something that can seriously be doubted if one is to continue in one's philosophical search for certainty? If Descartes really doubted what the senses told him, he wouldn't have bothered to write the *Meditations*. A genuine doubt about the existence of the physical world would mean that all actions and their consequences would be merely apparent and, therefore pointless, as we would not actually be achieving our aims. If we believed that in attempting to perform an action, we were, in fact, not performing it at all, then we would clearly need to completely re-evaluate our motives for performing actions in the first place.

Descartes' defence against this is that his philosophical doubt is purely theoretical and so need have no immediate impact on how he behaves (see the distinction between philosophical scepticism and ordinary scepticism on page 13). He believes it is possible to doubt for the sake of acquiring knowledge without putting action into question and so his scepticism needn't have any immediate practical consequences. Descartes is not concerned primarily with practical matters but rather with obtaining absolute certainty.

At the same time, however, we need to be clear that Descartes is not saying that his suspension of judgement is a purely academic exercise that could never have implications for his ordinary beliefs. On the contrary, if he finds good reason to reject his common-sense assumptions, he has resolved to do so. So is his doubt genuine or not? And how should it affect his actions? Descartes' answer is that until he has determined which beliefs are worthy of his assent, and which not, he cannot simply discard them all. The reason is that without them he would have nothing to guide his everyday conduct. He would effectively be paralysed, having no reason to do one thing rather than another. Consequently, he needs a set of rules by which to live until his sceptical meditations are complete. The ones to adopt are precisely the common-sense assumptions of his day – those beliefs he had accepted before he started doubting. In the absence of any other belief system, these remain the default option. In the *Discourse on Method*, Descartes proposed that, prior to discovering anything certain, he would:

Descartes

obey the laws and customs of my country, constantly retaining the religion which I judged best, and in which, by God's grace, I had been brought up since childhood, and in all other matters to follow the most moderate and least excessive opinions to be found in the practice of the most judicious part of the community in which I would live.[13]

In other words, the suspension of judgement about previous beliefs actually leaves a whole set of prejudices in place until they are refuted. These prejudices cannot be abandoned, since they are required for one to continue to live.

Hume's mitigated scepticism

Despite Descartes' defence, some philosophers have still complained that a doubt which has no practical implications is not really worthy of the name. The great Scottish philosopher David Hume (1711–76), for example, felt that genuine doubt would inevitably impact on how one lives. So if the sceptic claims to doubt that there is a dog before her, she should be consistent and not flinch when it leaps at her hand barking and snapping. If she *does* flinch, her action undermines her claim to doubt. Similarly, I might claim to doubt that you have a mind, but if I continue discussing my doubts with you, this shows how empty they are. We are just not capable of living out theoretical doubts about such fundamentals as the existence of our own bodies, other people and the physical objects that surround us.

Extreme scepticism in philosophy should therefore, as Hume had it, be *mitigated* or moderated by what we cannot help believing (MITIGATED SCEPTICISM). We possess certain natural dispositions which force us into holding certain beliefs, such as belief in the existence of our own bodies and the physical world. From a purely rational point of view, this may not be a fully justified hypothesis. We may not be able to find any rational arguments to defeat the sceptic. But here we don't need strong justification, because we are incapable of acting in any way other than in the complete conviction that there is a physical world. While *reason* appears to lead us into a sceptical hole, luckily our natural instincts or passions won't allow us to remain sceptical for long. So while reason may be useful for certain things, it has its limits. We cannot expect reason alone to give us sufficient grounds for us to claim knowledge of the physical world. If we were to wait for reason to do so, we would be paralysed, having no basis for action. Instead we need to put our faith in instinctive convictions.

So although the sceptic may seek to undermine our most natural and mundane beliefs, she must leave such argument to one side as soon as life demands action. Rather than produce a *rational* refutation of scepticism, something Hume regards as impossible, he relies on the inevitability of *nature* to undermine it. 'The great subverter of PYRRHONISM [i.e. scepticism]',[14] Hume wrote, 'is action, and employment, and the occupations of common life.'[15] In other words, nature does not allow one to choose to believe what reason would dictate. Hume attempts to defeat scepticism by this appeal to the overwhelming force of blind and natural impulses. Ultimately, this means that reason is not the dominant force in belief formation or in human life.[16]

The appeal to ordinary language

In everyday life we are happy to say that we are *certain* or that we *know* that grass is green, that dogs don't speak Chinese, and that Everest is the tallest mountain on earth, and we are rarely challenged when we do so. Ordinarily speaking, to see a table is good enough reason for affirming that one knows it exists. It is only philosophers who question our use of such words as 'know' and 'certain' in these and other contexts. They often claim that we need to refine our concepts of certainty and knowledge, and give them a philosophically strict meaning.

In the twentieth century, however, so-called ORDINARY LANGUAGE PHILOSOPHERS questioned this approach and in so doing hoped to find an alternative route to defeating the sceptic. So how does ordinary language philosophy attempt to overcome scepticism? To answer this question let's begin with the example of the term 'knowledge'. Remember that the sceptic claims that I cannot 'know', just because I *see* a table before me, that there really *is* a table before me. The possibility that there exist Cartesian demons or mad scientists deceiving us shows, according to the sceptic, that we cannot have knowledge of the nature or existence of the physical world. In other words, the sceptic argues that, because it is possible for me to be mistaken, I cannot really have knowledge.

Notice, however, that in ordinary language the merest possibility of error does not warrant avoiding the use of the words 'know' and 'knowledge'. In everyday life we say we know all kinds of things about which it is at least conceivable that we may be mistaken. For example, if in the ordinary course of things someone were to ask you if you *know* that there is a table before you, you would doubtless think she were joking. But if she were insistent that your knowledge claim might be ill-founded, you might be led to make some straightforward checks. You might make sure that it was no hologram by rapping your finger against it; or you might pick it up to ensure that it was indeed made of solid wood and not a fiendishly clever fake fashioned out of paper. Having conducted these tests you would – according to the ordinary use of the word – be quite justified in claiming that you *knew* that this thing was indeed a table. This is just the kind of situation in which the word 'know' or 'knowledge' is typically used. If the sceptic insists that you still do not know, even after these various checks have been made, then she is inviting you to buy into a radical departure from the way the word 'know' is normally used. This shows that the philosophical tradition uses the concept of knowledge (and of certainty, doubt, and so on) in a different way from our ordinary usage.

Having made this clear, the ordinary language philosopher can now claim that traditional sceptical arguments only have force if we accept this departure from our ordinary usage of terms like 'knowledge' and 'know'. But, the argument goes, the sceptic has given us no reason to accept this new usage. If we reject this departure and continue to use language in the ordinary way, then the sceptical arguments lose their force. Instead of responding to the sceptic by trying to prove that we really do know – even according to the new, stricter definition of knowledge – the ordinary language philosopher insists on keeping the old definition, and so can claim to know according to it.

But why should the ordinary usage of words like 'knowledge' be preferable? The ordinary language philosopher points out that words are meaningful because there is social agreement about their meaning. Words acquire their meaning from their use in everyday contexts. To rip them from those contexts and try to make them do work for which they are not designed is literally to start talking nonsense. Imagine trying to use the word 'biscuit' to do the work of the word 'the'. If others don't agree to accept your new usage, no one will understand you and you will very quickly start talking gobbledygook. You can't just use words to mean whatever you please. It's the same with philosophers who try to use words in the wrong way. In claiming to have grave doubts about the existence of physical objects, we have departed radically from ordinary usage of the word 'doubt' and in so doing we have raised confusions about how the

Ordinary language user

Philosopher

■ Figure 2.2
Language goes on holiday

Words like 'doubt' or 'know' begin life as ordinary words used in ordinary contexts. When being used in these contexts – when they are at home getting on with their everyday work – everyone understands how to use them and no puzzles arise. However, when words like these are taken out of their ordinary context – when they are taken off 'on holiday' by unscrupulous philosophers – they are no longer able to do the work for which they are suited and all sorts of confusions arise. The sceptic, when talking about 'knowledge', is no longer talking about the same thing that we are ordinarily talking about.

Here, the word 'doubt' is at home.

But here doubt has gone on holiday, which can lead to confusion.

word works. The sceptic is no longer talking about 'doubt', 'certainty', and 'knowledge', but rather about some peculiar philosophical versions of them.

In sum, philosophical doubt, by trading on the mere possibility of being mistaken, has little to do with the original or proper meaning. If we stick to the generally accepted understanding of the concept then the sceptic's argument is invalid.

The Austrian philosopher Ludwig Wittgenstein (1889–1951) claimed that all manner of philosophical muddles could be avoided if only people paid more attention to how language works in ordinary contexts. Philosophical difficulties arise when, as he put it, language is allowed to go on holiday, that is, when terms become used in inappropriate ways.

The appeal to common sense

In a similar move, philosophers have also tried to defeat scepticism by appealing to common sense. Again, the idea here is that philosophers are mistaken if they claim that we don't really know what we normally think we do. So the philosopher of common sense argues that the first task of any theory of knowledge is to account for the fact that we do know all kinds of ordinary things, rather than fabricate a peculiar philosophical definition of knowledge which drastically restricts what can be known.

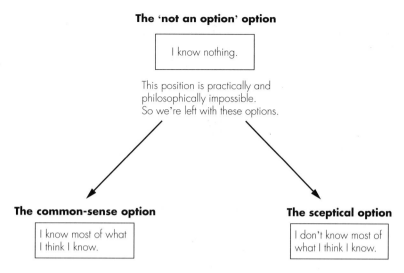

The 'not an option' option

> I know nothing.

This position is practically and
philosophically impossible.
So we're left with these options.

The common-sense option

> I know most of what
> I think I know.

The sceptical option

> I don't know most of
> what I think I know.

**■ Figure 2.3 *What
is more reasonable
to believe?***

*In life we don't really have
the option of believing
nothing at all. Rather we
have a choice about what
to believe. So the question
boils down to which
beliefs are more
reasonable. Given the
options, is it more
reasonable to believe that
we know most of what we
think we know, or that we
don't? The philosopher of
common sense argues that
we have compelling
reasons to believe
common sense rather than
what the sceptic offers.*

In the twentieth century, G. E. Moore (1873–1958)
pointed out that we have to take some beliefs for granted. We
can't hope to prove everything since the process would be
endless. As we saw above with the infinite regress of
justification, some beliefs must be basic and not in need of
any further proof. Moreover we cannot doubt everything at
once. Believing nothing is not a real option, since even the
sceptic has to retain some beliefs, for reasons we've discussed
above. So where does this leave us? Which things should we
believe? Well, why not believe the basic claims of common
sense? Don't these have as good a claim to our assent as any
other beliefs? And while it may well be that we cannot *prove*
them, this, for Moore, shows just how basic they are. Perhaps
they are so basic that they don't need to be proved, but
rather simply accepted. Moore argued that it is more
reasonable to believe common sense than any weird belief you
might be led to by doing too much philosophy.[17]

The defender of common sense argues that she knows
certain things (the existence of physical objects for instance)
even though she is unable to give any explicit justification for
the claim. We can, in other words, know things without
knowing how we know. At some point, she argues, we have
to accept that we reach rock bottom and doubting comes to
an end. The Scottish philosopher Thomas Reid (1710–96),
like Hume, recognised that anyone who took radical
scepticism seriously would be disabled from carrying out even
the most mundane day-to-day business. How can you be
certain that with the very next step you take the ground
won't collapse? How can you be sure this book won't
suddenly burst into flames as you turn the page? Scepticism,
taken seriously, would make every single act a leap into the

unknown. Since even the most committed sceptic has no trouble conducting their everyday affairs in their non-philosophical moments, we must assume that we are all incapable of sincere doubts about certain basic common-sense beliefs. Among these beliefs would be our conviction that the physical world exists and that it has the various properties that we perceive it to have, that other people have minds, and that the future will resemble the past. Such beliefs about the world, while not strictly provable rationally, are none the less so fundamental to our way of thinking as to be impossible to reject. Reid's point is that although it is possible (in one's theoretical moods) to raise doubts about the basic beliefs of common sense, they are not *doubt-worthy*, nor could anyone doubt them consistently. The assumptions of common sense are so basic to our lives that it is pointless to doubt them. They constitute the very fabric of our belief system and the merest possibility of being mistaken about them doesn't give us good reason to doubt them. In the absence of any good reason or evidence for us to doubt them we are justified in continuing to believe them. 'To what purpose is it for philosophy to decide against common sense in this or any other matter? The belief of a material world is older, and of more authority, than any principles of philosophy. It declines the tribunal of reason, and laughs at all the artillery of the logician.'[18]

Armed with the tools we have considered for defeating or moderating scepticism, consider the three sceptical arguments below. How might you defeat them? In constructing your case against these arguments, consider the following points:

- How might the arguments be self-defeating?
- Do they trade on a distinction, which they go on to deny?
- Do they presuppose knowledge, which they go on to claim is impossible?
- Do they depart from the ordinary use of language?
- Do they go against the basic tenets of common sense?

1 The light coming from the sun takes about six minutes to reach us. So what you are seeing when you glance up at the sun is actually an image of the sun as it was six minutes ago, not as it is now. So, it could be that the sun exploded five minutes ago and that what you are seeing no longer exists. Worse still, the same must go for the ordinary objects you see around you. For the light reflected from them takes some time to reach you, and in the interim they may have ceased to exist. It follows that you can't know that anything you see around you exists.

2 How can we be sure that any of the evidence we have about the past is reliable? Indeed, it is conceivable that the world came into existence only yesterday complete with apparent memories, history books and fossil records, all as a cosmic prank made up by some unthinkably powerful deity. Since we can't know that this hasn't happened, we can't have knowledge of the past. (Bertrand Russell, Lecture 9: 'Memory', *The Analysis of Mind*, Routledge 1989.)

3 We are becoming better and better at creating computers that can simulate reality. Virtual reality is often indistinguishable from the real thing. As our wizardry increases in sophistication, we can expect virtual reality machines to be able to mimic more and more aspects of our lives. Indeed, one day it may well be possible for the whole of one's life to be reproduced by some very fancy virtual reality machine. If this happened, once you were plugged into the machine you would no longer be able to tell the difference between living a virtual life and living a real life. But if this is right, then this may already have happened. Perhaps your life isn't real, but part of a virtual reality program created just for you. But if this is possible, then you can't be sure that any of your life is real.

Conclusion

In this chapter we've looked at different ways in which beliefs and knowledge claims can be justified, at how the philosophical sceptic casts doubt on such claims, and at different strategies for resisting or defeating scepticism. An important lesson to draw from all this is that the battle with scepticism is fought on a continuum between, on the one hand, the blind acceptance of beliefs, and on the other an extreme scepticism in which very little is accepted. If we are extremely gullible we'll believe all kinds of things and so have a large stock of beliefs. But gullibility is not a very sensible strategy in life or in philosophy. If we believe things on very little evidence then much of what we believe will be false. On the other hand, if we are overly sceptical, and refuse to believe things which are even slightly doubtful, then we'll end up believing very little. This is equally impractical as a strategy. If I harbour doubts about the reality of my body, or refuse to believe that the world will continue to obey the basic laws of physics, I will be unable to step out of my front door for fear that my legs may melt away beneath me, or that the pavement may turn into blancmange. The philosopher who refuses to believe anything ends up an incurable sceptic with a failed epistemology. So, it seems, in order to get on we need to decide where to operate on this continuum. How sceptical should we be? Where should we draw the line?

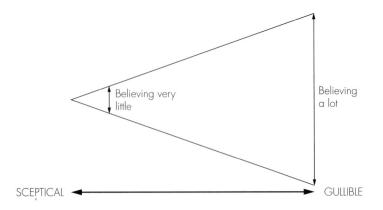

■ **Figure 2.4 How sceptical should we be?**

There is a continuum between the extremely sceptical and the extremely gullible. The more gullible one is, the more beliefs one can hold, the more sceptical the less. We have to decide whereabouts on this continuum we should arrest the sceptic.

Key points: Chapter 2

What you need to know about **knowledge and justification**:

1 Belief and knowledge claims require evidence that justifies one in believing them. Typically, beliefs are justified by appeals to one's own experience, to common knowledge, to the testimony of others, to other beliefs or are simply worked out by thinking.

2 Scepticism in philosophy is very different from scepticism in everyday life. It is an essential tool by which philosophers test their knowledge claims and how well they are justified, and try to determine what we can and cannot know.

3 The sceptic points out that the justification for any belief is infinitely long, suggesting that no belief is ultimately justified. The infinite regress of reasons seems to mean that nothing can be known.

4 Foundationalism is the traditional reaction to the scepticism of the infinite regress argument. It is the view that there must be certain basic beliefs that justify themselves and in terms of which all other beliefs are justified.

5 There are various further reactions to scepticism. Descartes' *cogito* argument, for example, appears to establish one's own existence beyond any possibility of doubt. Descartes hoped he could find further indubitable beliefs and so defeat the sceptic once and for all.

6 Some anti-sceptical arguments, termed 'transcendental', try to show that the sceptic presupposes what she tries to deny.

7 Others claim that global scepticism is self-defeating as one cannot consistently doubt all one's beliefs at once, doubt the nature of doubt itself, or doubt one's capacity to reason.

8 Ordinary language philosophers and philosophers of common sense try to defend our everyday belief system against the sceptic, claiming that it is more reasonable to believe what we ordinarily reckon is true than to allow the sceptic to persuade us that we actually know very little.

Rationalism, empiricism and the structure of knowledge

Introduction

We have seen that scepticism, and in particular the problem of the infinite regress of justification, has led philosophers to search for beliefs that cannot be doubted. Such beliefs do not need to be justified by appeal to any further beliefs, in other words they are self-evident or self-justifying. This approach to epistemology leads to the position known as *foundationalism*. Foundationalism is the view that divides our beliefs into two sets: those that need no further justification – the foundational ones – and those that do; what we can call the SUPERSTRUCTURAL ones, simply meaning those that are built on top of the foundations.

■ **Figure 3.1**
Foundationalism

Foundationalists see the structure of beliefs like a building with foundations supporting the superstructure. If we can find certain basic beliefs that cannot be doubted or which justify themselves, then all our other beliefs – the superstructural ones – can be secured on top of these foundations. In this way, all our beliefs will be securely justified in terms of the basic ones and so we would have a system of beliefs free from error.

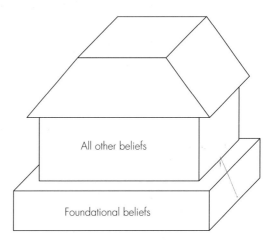

All other beliefs

Foundational beliefs

However, the pressing difficulty for foundationalism is to discover what these foundational beliefs are and what makes them self-justifying. What kind of beliefs could serve this function? In other words, what is the ultimate foundation for all knowledge? What is the bedrock in terms of which human knowledge is justified? Philosophers have disagreed about where these ultimate beliefs are to be found. During the seventeenth and eighteenth centuries two opposing schools of thought became established, each suggesting its own answer to these questions. The rationalists, based on the continent of

Europe, thought that all true knowledge should be based on reason. The empiricists, largely based in Britain, thought that all true knowledge must be based on the senses. This division has left a lasting impression that is still evident in the world of philosophy today. This chapter explores these two schools of thought, and examines their very different versions of foundationalism. We then go on to look at two alternative pictures of the nature of justification and of the structure of knowledge, namely *coherentism* and *reliabilism*. The chapter is divided as follows:

- The sources of knowledge
- Rationalism
- Empiricism
- Non-foundational accounts of knowledge
- Key points you need to know about rationalism, empiricism and the structure of knowledge.

The sources of knowledge

We all claim to know various facts about the world – the price of tomatoes, who wrote *Hamlet*, our birth dates, that 2 + 3 = 5. But where does this knowledge come from? Perhaps I learned who wrote *Hamlet* from a teacher at school. But where did the teacher gain their knowledge? Perhaps they got it from a book. But this simply leads us to the further question of where the author of the book gained their knowledge? In the end we are going to want to know what the original source for this piece of knowledge was.

experimenting with ideas

1 Make a copy of the table below. Using the word 'know' in its everyday sense, write down four things that you know in the left-hand column.

Then trace the knowledge back to its origin. Note the origin in the right-hand column.

2 Look at the origins of knowledge you have identified. Do they have anything in common? Are there any 'ultimate' sources of knowledge?

Something that you know	The origin of this piece of knowledge
1	
2	
3	
4	

Traditionally philosophers have identified four ultimate sources of knowledge. These are:

- Reason
- Experience
- Revelation
- Innate ideas.

Reason as the source of knowledge: rationalism

RATIONALISM is the view that the ultimate source of knowledge is reason. Rationalists often look to the world of mathematics as a template for their theory. Mathematical knowledge can be gained with reason alone and without the direct use of the senses. Alone in a room, cut off from the world, in theory it would be possible for me to work out substantial truths about geometric shapes and numbers just by thinking very hard. The knowledge that is gained in this way somehow appears to be eternal, or outside of time. In other words, while everything in the physical world comes in and out of existence, $2 + 3$ will always be 5. Moreover, mathematical knowledge seems to have a kind of certainty that exceeds other forms of knowledge. Knowledge that $2 + 3 = 5$ appears unshakable; it's difficult to see how one could be wrong about it. For these reasons, many rationalists thought that the model of mathematical knowledge, with its clarity and certainty, should be applied to all human knowledge. Through the application of reason, they argued, it would be possible to understand a significant body of knowledge about the world and how it operates. This knowledge, like that of maths, would be certain, logical and endure for all time. The evidence of the senses should agree with the truths of reason but they are not required for the acquisition of these truths.

The idea that the rationalists embody is also reflected in literature and myth. It is encapsulated in the image of the wise hermit who withdraws from the world and contemplates the deep questions of life and the universe. Through the application of reason and thought alone, the hermit slowly uncovers the essential truths about the world or the universal moral principles of life and so becomes exceedingly wise. The knowledge gained is not tainted by the ordinary concerns of everyday life and so has a kind of purity and eternity.

Experience as the source of knowledge: empiricism

EMPIRICISM is the view that the ultimate source of knowledge is experience. Empiricists argue that we are born knowing nothing. Everything we know, they claim, comes to us through our five senses. All our knowledge, indeed all our thoughts, must ultimately relate to things we have seen, smelt, touched, tasted or heard.

The spirit of empiricism is also embodied in literature and myth. Here we encounter the character of the wise traveller: someone who has set out and explored the world, has had many great and varied adventures, and finally returns with the wisdom of experience.

Revelation as the source of knowledge: gnosticism

Another view of the origins of human knowledge claims that genuine wisdom is only to be gained by means of divine revelation. This view is sometimes called gnosticism. Again, we find this idea personified in myth and literature in the figure of the mystic: a wise and deeply spiritual person to whom special knowledge is given, neither through the senses nor through reason, but from some supernatural source.

Innate ideas as the source of knowledge

Some philosophers believe that we are born knowing certain things, in other words we are born with *innate* knowledge. Is this true? It is undeniable that we are born with certain instincts: to suckle, to cry when hungry, and so on. However, whether these count as knowledge is debatable. After all, do swallows *know* that they must fly south in autumn? Do squirrels *know* that the winter is coming and that they should store nuts? It seems likely that they have no explicit understanding of these facts, but simply act instinctively. However, believers in innate knowledge argue that beyond instinct certain other elements, such as a moral sense, a knowledge of God, of abstract principles, or of mathematics, may also be known innately. The belief in INNATE KNOWLEDGE is traditionally associated with rationalism, since rationalists often felt that reason revealed knowledge that we were born with buried within our minds.

For the purposes of this chapter we will be focusing on the first two sources of knowledge: reason and experience. However, since rationalists, such as Descartes, explain the possibility that much knowledge is discoverable by reason by claiming that it is innate, the issue of whether we are born with innate ideas won't be far away from the discussion. Note that rationalism and empiricism as characterised here are extreme positions, and that few, if any, philosophers can be characterised as purely rationalist or purely empiricist. Rather, we should think of these terms as poles on a spectrum on which we can place different philosophers.

Rationalism

Descartes can be placed on the rationalist end of this spectrum. Rather than rely on the senses, he uses reason to find the certainties on which he hopes to rebuild his body of knowledge. As we have seen, the first such certainty is the *cogito* (page 23). But impressive as it may be, the *cogito* is a pretty limited place to start to rebuild a body of knowledge. Descartes needs further truths which also have this character of being self-justifying and which can be known just by thinking about them. Are there any other truths that have this quality? Descartes thinks there are and he calls them 'CLEAR AND DISTINCT IDEAS'. These ideas, we are told, are ideas that can be 'intuited' by the mind by what he calls the 'light of reason'. They are truths of *reason*, truths that can be known with the mind alone. Descartes' examples of self-justifying beliefs are the basic claims of logic, geometry and mathematics. Such knowledge, it is claimed, resists any sceptical attack, since we recognise its truth immediately. Our faculty of INTUITION permits us to recognise the truth of such propositions without allowing any room for doubt or error. It is in vain to ask how I know that triangles have three sides. Such knowledge is given in the very act of understanding the terms involved. There is no further evidence I could appeal to which could justify such knowledge.[19]

So here we appear to have found one candidate for the foundations for which we were searching. Truths of reason are the bedrock on which we might build the whole of human knowledge, and importantly, knowledge of the physical universe around us. The infinite regress of justification ends with Descartes' 'clear and distinct ideas'. According to this view, knowledge of the world has the following structure:

■ **Figure 3.2**
Descartes'
foundationalism

All knowledge is based on a foundation of beliefs. These beliefs are knowable a priori, and are self-justifying – they are called 'clear and distinct ideas'. The rest of our beliefs, principally those about the physical world, are to be justified in terms of these basic beliefs.

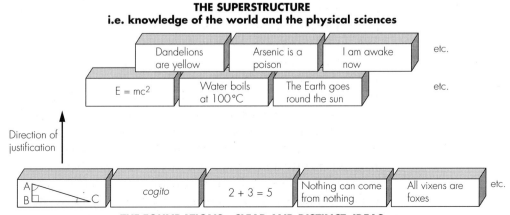

THE SUPERSTRUCTURE
i.e. knowledge of the world and the physical sciences

| Dandelions are yellow | Arsenic is a poison | I am awake now | etc. |

| $E = mc^2$ | Water boils at 100°C | The Earth goes round the sun | etc. |

Direction of justification

| A B C | *cogito* | $2 + 3 = 5$ | Nothing can come from nothing | All vixens are foxes | etc. |

THE FOUNDATIONS: 'CLEAR AND DISTINCT' IDEAS
i.e. knowledge of my existence, of maths and geometry; truths of reason and analytic truths

A *priori* knowledge and *a posteriori* (empirical) knowledge[20]

more difficult

'Clear and distinct ideas' – the kinds of belief which can be known just by thinking about them – are often termed A PRIORI. This means that they can be recognised *prior* to or independently of experience. So I don't need to check whether triangles have three sides by first finding a triangle and then counting the sides. I can tell what the answer will be before (i.e. *prior* to) conducting any such experiment. Similarly, I can know in advance that no matter in what pattern I arrange five marbles (in two groups of four and one; two groups of two and three, or three groups of two, two and one, and so on) the total number will remain five. Of course, I have to know the meanings of the terms involved here to recognise such truths, but this is all. Truths that are not from mathematics or geometry can also be known *a priori*. We can know without having to check that if an object is blue all over it cannot also be orange. This is just how colours work.

Another kind of belief that can be known *a priori* is one that is true by definition. Take, for example, the proposition: 'All spinsters are female'. I don't need to conduct a survey of spinsters to justify my belief that this is true. I would be wasting my time if I did. To take another example, contrast the proposition: 'No one can steal the Queen of England's property' with 'No one can steal his or her own property'. In the first case, to establish whether or not it is true I would have to make various enquiries into the security surrounding the Queen. So establishing its truth would involve more than just thinking about the meaning of the proposition. But in the second case, I can see that it must be true just by understanding what the terms involved mean. It is impossible to steal one's own property just because stealing means taking someone else's property (without permission). No further investigation is necessary. Truths such as these, which can be recognised as true simply through an examination of the meanings of the terms involved, are termed ANALYTIC.

A priori beliefs are to be contrasted with those that can be justified only after having had further evidence, that is through experience. Such knowledge is termed A POSTERIORI or *empirical* knowledge. Knowing that no one can steal the Queen's property would be a piece of *a posteriori* knowledge. Similarly, I can come to know only through experience whether apples are tasty, or if spinsters are miserable. Truths such as these depend on the way the world happens to be. Empirical knowledge is the province of the natural sciences, such as physics and chemistry, and so includes knowledge of so-called 'laws of nature'.

Plato and the theory of forms

The fascination with *a priori* truths, especially those of mathematics and geometry, and the tendency to regard them as in some way superior to *a posteriori* truths has a long philosophical history. To regard such knowledge as having a privileged status, and to hold it as a benchmark for all other knowledge claims, is one of the main features of rationalism. In this Descartes is in the good company of Plato (*c.* 428–347BC). Plato is regarded by many as the most important of the Ancient Greek philosophers and as the father of the whole of western philosophy. Both he and Descartes, two thousand years later, contended that knowledge had to involve self-evidence, and this possibility is fulfilled most effectively by beliefs acquired *a priori*. What particularly impresses rationalists about a geometric proof, for example, is that once one sees its truth one also recognises that no further evidence could undermine it. It is a truth that appears unchanging and eternal and which couldn't be otherwise. For example, consider the following proof that Plato employs in his dialogue, the *Meno*:

■ **Figure 3.3**
Socrates' experiment with the slave in Plato's Meno
This diagram shows that the total area of the square EFGH is twice that of the square ABCD. This can clearly be seen since each of the four triangles (1, 2, 3 and 4) which divide ABCD is equal in area and equal to each of the eight triangles (1, 2, 3, 4, 5, 6, 7 and 8) which divide EFGH, and eight is twice four.[21]

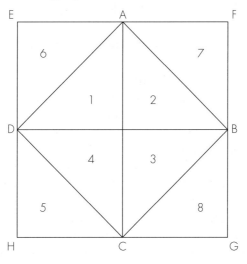

Once the proof is understood, one recognises it to be true not just of the particular square drawn on the page but of all squares, indeed of squares as such. This suggested to Plato that such knowledge cannot derive from our experience, since our experience is only ever of particular squares. So how is such an understanding possible? Plato's answer was that the mind sees the essential nature or FORM of the square and recognises truths about this, rather than about the particular example of a square one sees with one's eyes. Like Descartes he thought that we have an innate faculty which recognises such truths as eternal and necessary. This furnishes us with genuine knowledge. By contrast, our understanding of empirical truths learned *a posteriori* lacks such certainty. They are only ever *contingently* true, that is to say, they might not have been true and only happen to be true. For this reason, we can only have beliefs about them.

Moreover, the precise properties of geometric and mathematical ideas are never found among physical objects, since never in the physical world do we encounter perfect circles or squares, or numbers. At some level of detail, all examples of circles are only approximately circular. Only the form of 'circle' is perfectly or unqualifiedly circular. All threesomes come and go in the physical world, but the number three is timeless and eternal. It does not exist in time or space and so cannot undergo any changes. By contrast, even the most enduring of physical objects is both located in space and subject to change over time. This kind of consideration leads Plato to suppose that mathematics and geometry attain to precision and certainty to the extent that they do not apply to objects in the physical world. Since he thinks they must none the less apply to something, he posits a realm of intelligible objects which is more real than this world of imperfect, changeable objects.

In this way Plato draws a distinction between a world of ideal forms – the object of knowledge – and the physical world of which only belief or opinion is possible. But in Plato's mind knowledge isn't restricted to maths and geometry. We can acquire knowledge of the essential nature of moral and aesthetic concepts, such as justice and beauty, in the same way, by contemplating the essential nature of them with the mind. This is because the idea or form of beauty exists independently of any particular beautiful things, just as the form of the square exists independently of square things. Physical things may be beautiful to some degree, but cannot be completely or perfectly beautiful. Their beauty comes and goes, and always depends on factors such as the state of the perceiver, the context, and so forth. Yet we can acquire knowledge of the eternal and unchanging form of beauty by reasoning about the concept in an *a priori* manner.

Plato contrasts forms and sensible objects by saying the former are 'forever', or 'always are', whereas the latter 'wander in generation and decay',[22] meaning that while objects are subject to change, the form is unalterable. Plato uses a variety of metaphors to describe the relation that obtains between the two worlds. Sometimes he speaks of the form being 'present' in an object, or of the object 'sharing in' the form. Alternatively, he speaks of the object as an 'approximation', 'copy' or 'imitation' of the form.[23] The form may also be thought of as like a mould or blueprint determining what a set of objects of a certain kind have in common, while no two particulars need ever be identical. It is our recognition of the form in the particular which enables us to see that it belongs to a certain class of thing.

1 Read through the following statements.

2 Decide whether you believe/know them *a priori* or *a posteriori*.

a) Everyone wants what is good.

b) The square root of 81 is 9.

c) All bachelors are unmarried men.

d) Some bachelors have penthouses and throw wild parties.

e) Mammals exist which have beaks like ducks, and which lay eggs.

f) God exists.

g) All things eventually decay and die.

h) Material objects occupy space.

i) Two parallel lines will never meet.

j) Nothing can come from nothing.

Scepticism about the nature and extent of rational knowledge

▶ criticism ◀ Few philosophers today would agree that we can acquire the precision of mathematical knowledge in aesthetics or morals. Concepts of justice and beauty are vague and may vary between individuals and cultures. But what of scientific knowledge? Descartes reckoned it would be possible to work out basic physical laws with mathematical certainty simply by reasoning from indubitable first principles without empirical observation. However, this project now seems overly ambitious. His difficulty was how to move from knowledge of his own existence and of *a priori* truths to that of the physical world. Mathematical truths may be eternal and necessary, but they can't be used to overcome scepticism about the existence of the world, nor can maths and geometry alone tell us how it behaves. To know that if I have two marbles and then add three more marbles that I will have five, tells me nothing about whether or not there are marbles.[24] The price of asking that all our knowledge come through reason seems to be that we wind up not knowing very much.

Another way to argue this point is to claim that reason alone can tell us only about *analytic* truths. Analytic truths are true by definition, truths which cannot be denied without contradiction. For example, it is analytically true that a square has four sides. To say that a square does not have four sides is to contradict oneself. Contrasted with analytic truths are SYNTHETIC truths, which are not true simply by definition and can be denied without contradiction. For example, it is a synthetic truth that the dinosaurs died out, or that the sky is blue. Dinosaurs might have continued to dominate the Earth

– perhaps if the asteroid that wiped them out had been on a slightly different course and had missed the Earth. The sky could have been yellow, say, if the atmosphere had been made of a different gas. These possibilities are conceivable since there is no contradiction in them.

It is often claimed that all truths about the physical world, all empirical truths, are synthetic in this sense. This means that even the truth that gravity pulls objects down toward the centre of the Earth is synthetic. Even the laws of physics could have been different. Crucially, because their denial cannot be seen to be false just by thinking about it, they cannot be discovered to be true by reason alone. So, I cannot work out the laws of physics, just as I cannot work out what colour the sky is, by reason alone. Such things can be found out only by observation. This is an argument put forward by the empiricist philosopher David Hume. It is important because, if it is right, it shows that reason is of limited use. Experience can be the only true source of knowledge about the physical universe.

Other rationalists

Hume's claim is that the rationalist enterprise must fail. It fails because reason will provide us only with necessary truths, truths that could not be otherwise, whereas knowledge of the world involves knowledge of CONTINGENT truths – truths that could have been otherwise. However, Descartes was not the only rationalist of the modern era. Others followed in his footsteps and took up the challenge of establishing knowledge through reason. Two of these, Leibniz and Spinoza, avoid Hume's criticism to some extent since both of them claimed that all empirical truths are necessary, and so, in principle, can be established by reason alone.

more difficult

■ Leibniz

Gottfried Wilhelm von Leibniz (1646–1716), like Descartes, was another great polymath. Most of his life was spent working in the courts of various European royalty and consequently his studies in philosophy, maths and science were all conducted in his spare time. Much of his philosophy was carried out with correspondents through the exchange of letters – he wrote over 16,000 in his lifetime. He was also a great mathematician and discovered calculus at the same time as Isaac Newton. Leibniz established a complex and contained metaphysical view of the world and it is very easy to misrepresent his views by presenting small segments of his philosophy in isolation. Leibniz believed that God existed *necessarily* and that by definition God is all-good, all-powerful and all-knowing. He subscribed to a version of what is known as the 'ontological argument' for the existence of God. In outline, this argument claims that if we understand the concept of God properly we will recognise that he just has to exist, that is, his existence is necessary. Since this necessary being is all-good and all-powerful, it follows that the world he created would have to be the best possible world there could be. It would be nonsensical for an all-good and all-powerful God to create a less than perfect world. So the world we live in, and every event that takes place in it, takes place necessarily as part of the divine plan to maximise the good.[25]

This may seem implausible initially. We can see perfectly well that a lot of what goes on in the world is not good. We can certainly imagine far better worlds than this one – for example, worlds without famine, or the suffering of innocent children. Leibniz defends himself against this objection by arguing that the apparent imperfections in this world appear only because we have a limited view of the whole of God's creation. Each local piece of evil is necessary in order to maximise the overall perfection of the world. So some suffering is required so that more good can be realised, just as we must sometimes endure the discomfort of taking unpleasant medicine in order to recover from an illness. If we had the mind of God and could grasp the bigger picture, we would see that these apparent imperfections are necessary and so could understand the reason for everything in the universe. So, in principle at least, all empirical truths about the world could be worked out *a priori*, just by thinking about them. So, we wouldn't need to do any empirical research to know whether there will be a white Christmas this year. We could work it out, just by thinking about whether a white Christmas would be part of God's plan to produce the best possible world. Of course, in reality, humans are not up to the task of working out truths like this by reason alone. Our finite minds can't see whether snow or no snow would be best. This is why we have to do empirical research and why such truths appear contingent.

Spinoza

Benedict de Spinoza (1632–77) was born in Amsterdam. He lived an austere life, refusing to accept his inheritance and earning his living as a humble lens-grinder. He died, in February 1677, of consumption, probably triggered by the fine glass dust that he inhaled every day. While grinding he would contemplate philosophical ideas, often discussing his thoughts with friends and intellectuals who would frequent his workshop. Spinoza, like Descartes and Leibniz, adopted the rationalist view that the essential truths about the world should be established through reason and thus could attain the certainty of maths and geometry. His great work, *The Ethics*, starts by stating a series of definitions and axioms that he believes cannot be doubted. Inspired by the geometric method of Euclid who, using a few axioms and definitions, proves various geometrical propositions, Spinoza proceeds to try to deduce in the same manner all sorts of general or metaphysical truths. As *The Ethics* develops, Spinoza arrives at a strange and complex metaphysical picture of the world. Spinoza was a pantheist, believing that God is one and the same as the universe and, like Leibniz, he claimed that all truths are NECESSARY and nothing is contingent. The appearance of contingency is the result of the fact that our minds are not powerful enough to see why everything is the way it is. Forming only a small part of the universe, each human fails to see how every part of the universe, i.e. God, is connected, and it is from this that the feeling of contingency arrives. So while it may seem to me that some events in the universe just happen to be the case, in fact all are necessary. I had to have the cup of tea I've just finished, as this was a necessary event. I couldn't have had a cup of coffee instead.[26]

▶ criticism ◀ The rationalist views adopted by both Leibniz and Spinoza avoid Hume's criticism by claiming that the truths about the world are necessary rather than contingent, and so could, in theory, be discovered by reason. However, these attempts at the rationalist enterprise raise further difficulties. Chiefly, both accounts claim that every event is necessary through their conception of God as a necessary being, who in turn, confers necessity on the world. As such, they rely on the existence of God, and although both attempt to prove the existence of God using reason alone, neither of their versions of the ontological argument is generally considered successful.[27]

However, we could try to imagine a modern-day version of rationalism, which posits a necessary universe that does not rely on the existence of God. We can already predict successfully the movements of the moon and the planets by applying the relevant scientific laws to some initial starting positions. We can also predict the outcome of thousands of chemical reactions in the same way. Now, imagine this predictive power extended a million-fold, such that the behaviour of every atom could be predicted using the laws of nature and initial starting conditions. (Let us assume that there is no random element in nature, and that we are able to surmise initial starting conditions of particles down to the sub-atomic level.) Imagine further that we can somehow find out the exact starting conditions of the universe at the Big Bang. We would have a situation where, theoretically, some sort of super-computer could predict how every event in the universe subsequently took place, right up to and including the event of your reading this now.

more difficult

This thought experiment suggests a way that reason (albeit through a computer) could indeed work out all truths about the universe. However even this scenario (which contains many dubious assumptions) fails to live up to the rationalist ideal. How could reason alone work out the laws of nature and the initial starting conditions of the universe? These would have to be established through the senses, through observing how the universe works. An out-and-out rationalist would have to claim that these too could be established using reason alone, by claiming that there is only one logically possible universe and set of natural laws that could exist. Yet this view is hard to believe – surely this isn't the only possible universe. Things could have been different. It is hard to see how a universe in which I drank a cup of coffee five minutes ago instead of the cup of tea I in fact had, is *logically* impossible. Further, current science even suggests that universes with different laws of nature may be possible. So it seems that no matter how hard we push the case, it is simply not possible to prove substantial truths about the universe and the way it works by using reason alone.

The legacy of rationalism

The idea of seeking the truth through reason and establishing absolute certainty is an attractive proposition that has tempted many philosophers; some no doubt spurred on by the clarity and precision with which the truths of maths and geometry were established. It is perhaps no coincidence that many of the great rationalists were also great mathematicians. But it seems that although pure reason works very well in that sphere it cannot do the same for science and the world. For example, no matter how hard I consider the issue, I will not be able to work out how long it will take for an object with a particular mass to fall from a tower. To find out I will need to go and time it, and so experimentation is a necessary starting point for scientific knowledge.

However, the rationalist enterprise has not been without importance. First, the early rationalists were attempting to apply reason to a whole range of religious and spiritual questions in a way that had not been attempted since the Greeks, and were often in trouble with the religious authorities for doing so. However, it is their work that helped to lead the way for others and to make the application of reason to all areas of existence both acceptable and exciting.

But rationalism, and in particular Descartes, is important for another reason. Before Descartes, philosophers would often start out with a belief about the world and what it is like (an ONTOLOGY), and this belief would then determine what would count as knowledge. Much western philosophy in the centuries leading up to Descartes was concerned largely with theological issues that were often quite obscure in their nature. The philosophy of this period is sometimes characterised by the slur that philosophers were simply debating trivialities, such as how many angels can fit on the head of a pin. Whatever the merits of these debates, it is undeniable that they took for granted the existence of God and would then exercise reason around this core conviction. In other words, the philosophers placed their belief about what exists at the centre of their philosophy. Plato, similarly, allowed his theory that there were two worlds, a world of forms and the physical world, to determine what counts as true knowledge.

However, Descartes wanted to start anew. He believed that the correct order in which to undertake philosophy was first to establish how knowledge could be acquired, and only then proceed to establish truths about the world. His method is to accept only clear and distinct ideas, and then to proceed on their basis. Although Descartes may not have established a large body of certain truths through his rationalist enterprise, his focus on method and putting epistemology first has had a lasting impact. The emphasis on method became incorporated into science and has helped science become what it is. Treating epistemology as first philosophy is also what defines modern philosophy and is one of the reasons why Descartes is regarded as its father.

■ Summary of the advantages and disadvantages of rational knowledge

Advantages	Disadvantages
Rational truths are:	But reason:
■ eternally true	■ gives no knowledge of contingent truths
■ necessary	■ gives no empirical knowledge
■ known just by thinking	■ gives no knowledge of natural sciences.
■ self-justifying.	

Empiricism

If all of our knowledge does not come from reason perhaps it comes from *experience*. This is the basic idea behind the approach to philosophy known as empiricism. In its most basic form, empiricism claims that we are all born knowing nothing and that everything we know must come from our senses. To see how this is supposed to work we need first to make clear an important distinction between sense experiences and CONCEPTS. Much of what we are conscious of is what we are actually sensing. So I am now aware of the coffee I am drinking because I am actually seeing, tasting and smelling it. But I am also able to think about coffee when I am not actually in its presence. This is an important ability since without it we would only ever be conscious of what we are sensing at the present moment. If we couldn't think about things such as coffee while we were not actually drinking it then we could not recognise it on the next occasion, nor could we hold any beliefs about it, such as that it is a good drink to wake up to, or that it is made from ground and roasted beans. So concept formation is crucial to knowing about the world. Understanding its mechanism is going to be central to any epistemology.

Empiricism claims that all our concepts, like that of coffee, are formed out of sense experiences. It's only because I have encountered coffee that I can have the concept of coffee, and so can form beliefs about it. At first glance, this view seems inadequate to account for the complexity of the mind, since we surely possess all kinds of concepts of things we have never experienced. For example, we are able to imagine all kinds of fantasy creatures, such as unicorns and dragons, that don't exist in reality and which we have never encountered. I am able to imagine green aliens with eyes on stalks and spiky legs, which I have never actually witnessed with my senses. However, on closer inspection I have to concede that the elements out of which I have composed my imaginary alien do indeed come from my own experiences. Its colour is derived from my perception of grass and leaves; the antennae are obtained from seeing butterflies; and its spiky legs are stolen from crabs I observed on the beach. It seems that all the elements of my imaginary alien friend have, in one way or another, come from my sense experience of the world. The only novel thing is the arrangement of the elements. And so it goes, argues the empiricist, with anything I can imagine or conceive.[28]

ACTIVITY   Consider the following questions.

1 Is it possible to imagine a colour you have never experienced before?

2 Do you think someone who is colour blind from birth could ever know what red is?

3 Construct your own alien or made-up creature and then identify how your construction is derived from experience.

4 Can you think of any ideas that are not ultimately derived from experience?

5 Do your answers to these questions tend to support empiricism? Or do they raise difficulties with it?

Traditional empiricism claims that our imaginations can rearrange the basic elements we acquire from experience but we cannot invent these elements for ourselves. This leads to the following picture of the contents of our minds. There are, on the one hand, sense impressions or SENSE DATA. These are the basic elements that come into the mind through the senses, and cannot be broken down further into smaller elements. Examples of simple sense experiences might be the sight of red, the smell of coffee, or the sound of a trumpet. On the other hand, we can also think about the things we experience when we are not actually perceiving them. I can think of the colour red or a nice cup of coffee even when I'm not presently experiencing them: in other words I can form concepts. To do this, according to the empiricist, the mind retains the basic sense experience as a kind of copy or image. This copy is stored in the mind so that we can think about things we are not experiencing and recognise them when we encounter them. For example, I acquire the concept of red from first observing it and my mind stores the concept as a kind of image of the original sensation. Armed with this concept, I am able to recognise some new experience as being an experience of red. In the same way, my concept of coffee is formed from the various sense experiences I have had of coffee from seeing, smelling and tasting it. My concept of coffee, therefore, unlike that of red, is complex, since it is formed out of the various simple elements of its smell, colour, taste and so forth. Once I have the concept of coffee, the next time I encounter some coffee I can recognise it. Having the concept of coffee also enables me to distinguish it from tea. Simple concepts, like red, can be acquired only if one has experienced them. So a blind person cannot have the concept of red because they haven't had the sense datum of red. But, as we've seen, I can concoct new, complex concepts of things I have never experienced by rearranging simple elements.

The certainty of sensation or 'sense data'

In the previous chapter we saw that an attractive response to someone who is being sceptical about our beliefs is to claim certainty of those things of which we have had direct experience. This is borne out in everyday life. In response to the question, 'How do you know?' we frequently use answers such as 'Because I was there' or 'Because I saw it'. Similarly, in the short dialogue on page 12 we saw this tendency in Laura's responses. She hopes to arrest the sceptical questioning by appealing to her own investigations. She can be more certain of the truth about Amazon crocodiles because she has seen them herself, and doesn't have to rely on the testimony of others.

So it seems we are often inclined to appeal to our own personal experience when attempting to justify our claims to know things, and this is one point that empiricists stress. However, we have also encountered reasons to be sceptical about the reliability of the senses as a source of justification for our beliefs. Descartes argued that the senses may not be a secure basis for knowledge about the world and pointed to their susceptibility to error. Other considerations such as the possibility of sense deception, hallucinations and dreaming further undermined their reliability. In the worst-case scenario he even claimed that an evil demon could be giving me the sensations I'm having. Also the brain in a vat possibility on page 18 can serve to undermine the certainty of our senses. So it seems that, despite what we might ordinarily think, our own experience of the evidence of the senses is not a firm bedrock, and so could not function as the foundation of knowledge.

However, even if we accept that our senses may deceive us about the world, it seems impossible to deny that we are actually having sense experiences. Whether or not the world exists, I remain conscious of having various sensations. I may be hallucinating or be in a virtual reality machine and thus the purple curtains I am staring at may not actually exist, but despite all this it seems impossible to deny that I am having a purple-curtain-like experience. I'll grant the sceptic that the physical world is a figment of my imagination, but the sceptic still cannot take away the fact that I am now having an experience (albeit in imagination alone) of purple.

As Descartes puts it, even if I am dreaming, 'all the same, at least, it is very certain that *it seems to me* that I see light, hear a noise and feel a heat; and this is properly what in me is called perceiving'.[29] Thus to the extent that sensation or 'perceiving' is treated purely as an aspect of conscious experience, and any judgement about the nature of the world

53

beyond it is suspended, then it has a kind of certainty. This means that while I can doubt the existence of the physical universe, I cannot doubt the existence of the sensations which present themselves to me.

This is a crucially important move for the development of modern philosophy. Descartes' genius was to recognise that even if the entire physical world is a dream, or if there is an evil demon deceiving me, none the less sensations can be viewed purely as an aspect of consciousness. This means that the experience of sensation need not commit us to any beliefs concerning the material things which we may normally associate with it, i.e. our bodies' sense organs and the effects made on them by physical objects. So I can know I'm experiencing sensations regardless of whether or not objects or even my body really exist. Indeed, Descartes would even say that I can know with absolute certainty that I have a headache, even though I may not know that I have a head!

The incorrigibility of sensation

Now, if my own sensations are certain, regardless of any doubts that may be raised about their origin, then it seems that I cannot be led to change my mind about them. There is no new evidence which could come to light, in other words, which could lead me to correct my claim to know that I am having a sensation of a certain sort – be it seeing a purple patch, experiencing a smell of lavender, or suffering from a headache. I know I am having them whether or not purple things, lavender or even my own head exist. I cannot be brought to doubt that I have a headache no matter what sceptical scenarios one might raise. And the question, 'How do you *know* you have a headache?' seems a silly one.

It is on the basis of our sensations that we infer the existence of objects and events, mostly without being aware of doing so. I open the fridge and have a yellow and round visual experience – from this I infer there is a grapefruit before me. I have a barking aural experience, and infer the existence of a dog outside. In these cases we move from our basic sense experience to a belief about the world. In moving from one to the other there is the possibility of error: it may be a toy grapefruit; it may be a dog impersonator outside my window. I may even be dreaming. Because there is an inference involved, there is always room for doubt. But when it comes to experiencing the sensations themselves no inference is necessary. They are presented immediately to my mind and so knowledge of them allows no room for error. That I am experiencing a yellow, round shape cannot be doubted, regardless of what is actually causing it.

It seems that we have indeed found a second bedrock of beliefs. Those about our own sensations are immune from sceptical doubts and for this reason are often termed INCORRIGIBLE; meaning that they are not correctable. I would not under any conceivable circumstances give them up. In other words, they require no further justification; they are, as it is often put, simply GIVEN. Sensations treated simply as aspects of consciousness are often termed sense data, or sometimes the given.

The idea that all knowledge can finally be justified in terms of immediate experience leads into a second kind of foundationalism, namely empiricist foundationalism. The empiricist foundationalist doesn't think all knowledge can be justified in terms of self-evident truths of reason as the rationalist does, but rather thinks that what is given in experience – the certainties of my own sense data – are the true foundation of human knowledge.

Locke and empiricism

What this came to mean for empiricists like the English philosopher John Locke (1632–1704) is that all experience and all human knowledge can be analysed into simple data of SENSATION. These are the elements out of which experience is constructed. The classic expression of this idea is found in Locke's *Essay Concerning Human Understanding* (1690). The elements of experience which Locke has in mind are simple sensations of, to use his examples, whiteness and hardness.[30] When we are born, Locke claims, our minds are completely empty of any concepts or beliefs, both of which he terms 'ideas', and it is through experience that our minds become furnished. In one image, he tells us that the mind is originally akin to a blank piece of paper void of all characters – it is a *tabula rasa* or blank slate onto which our experience through life writes.

Knowledge of sense data

Although we have not yet discussed the concept of knowledge in detail or looked at the different sorts of knowledge that there are (we're saving this for Chapter 5), it's worth looking ahead a little at this point, for the kind of knowledge we have of sense data is, in an important way, unlike other sorts of knowledge. One sort of knowledge involves believing facts, expressed in sentences, and so is usually called factual knowledge (sometimes it is called propositional knowledge – a proposition being another word for a factual sentence). For example, I might know that snow is made of crystals, or that Elton John's real name is Reginald Dwight. Such knowledge is often gained from books, teachers or TV. As such we *infer* the knowledge from the relevant sources or from our other beliefs. However, our knowledge of sense data is different in that it is immediate and present, and not inferred from anything else. We may subsequently use the awareness of the sense data to infer the existence of objects and things, but the sense data themselves are given immediately to us – they do not have to be inferred. We are immediately acquainted with them and so I can know I am having a certain sense datum without having to justify it by reference to any other claim. So we have here a distinction between factual knowledge, which is inferred, and knowledge by acquaintance, which is not.

■ **Figure 3.4**
Empiricist
foundationalism

The empiricist foundationalist regards knowledge of sensations or sense data as the basis for all our factual knowledge about the world. Knowledge of sense data is immediate and incorrigible. On this basis we infer the existence of the physical world. So all our knowledge of the physical world is ultimately justified in terms of knowledge about our own sense data.

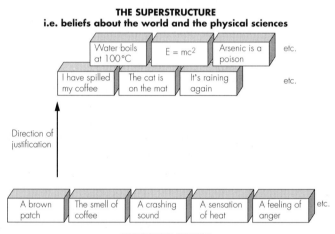

THE SUPERSTRUCTURE
i.e. beliefs about the world and the physical sciences

Water boils at 100°C $E = mc^2$ Arsenic is a poison   etc.

I have spilled my coffee   The cat is on the mat   It's raining again   etc.

Direction of justification

A brown patch   The smell of coffee   A crashing sound   A sensation of heat   A feeling of anger   etc.

THE FOUNDATIONS
Things we are immediately aware of such as colours, sounds and smells, as well as emotions and feelings; sometimes referred to as 'sense data' or the 'given'.

Now, we can use this distinction between inferred and immediate knowledge to clarify what the empiricist foundationalist is saying. Essentially, the idea is that the knowledge one has of one's own sense data is incorrigible because one is directly acquainted with it. It is the bedrock on which all other knowledge must be based since it involves an immediate awareness. For this reason I cannot be mistaken into thinking that I am acquainted with a certain smell when in fact I am not. Notice however that such knowledge does not require that we are able to say anything about the experience in question. Thus, if I have toothache I am intimately acquainted with a pain, but I may not know that I have a wisdom tooth coming through. That is, I may know very little about my condition. Knowledge by acquaintance in itself remains incommunicable since it lacks what is often called PROPOSITIONAL CONTENT. In other words, while factual

more
difficult

knowledge can be expressed in a PROPOSITION, knowledge by acquaintance need not be. So I can know I have a toothache simply by being acquainted with it, but not be able to say anything about it. A dentist, on the other hand, may know all kinds of things about my toothache and be able to communicate them to me and others in the form of propositions. In this sense, factual knowledge appears to be objective, while knowledge by acquaintance is subjective. So the empiricist foundationalist's idea is that factual knowledge about the world can be built on top of the incorrigible knowledge by acquaintance.

Hume and empiricism

Hume didn't just think that empiricism provided the correct account of how we gain knowledge, but also, like Locke before him, that it could shed important light on a great many philosophical problems. It would do this because the empiricist theory of the source and justification of knowledge also gave an account of what kinds of concept we can legitimately have, and the kinds of claims we can truly know. In other words, it provided a tool by which we could distinguish those things of which we could hope to acquire knowledge from those we could not.

To see how this works, recall that the empiricists are saying that any concept I have must be able to trace its origins back to the sensations or emotions from which it derives. So, consider the concept of a unicorn. Where does this concept come from? If it is a genuine concept it must be able to trace its origins back to sensation. In this case, the complex concept is composed of our concepts of a horse and a horn, and these ultimately derive from experience of horses and horns. In a similar way, the concept of tournament derives from experience of the teams and the matches they play. In the process of tracing concepts back to experience, their true nature is revealed and we may find that some are rather different from what we had supposed. Only once we are clear about the true nature of our concepts can we hope to make philosophical progress.

More radically, it sometimes occurs that we fail to trace a concept back to experience. According to Hume, if we cannot find the origins of an idea or concept, then in effect it cannot be a concept at all. So what is it then? Hume's answer is that it is a kind of error. We may think we have a concept because we have a word and the word seems to be the sign for a concept. But when we look closely we may discover that it was not a concept at all. Such apparent concepts are to be treated with suspicion and rejected as confusions.

This point is most obvious if we consider a made-up word like 'wagglytoth'. We have no idea of what a wagglytoth is because we cannot trace any such concept back to sensations or emotions. We have nothing to 'picture', as it were, when we use the word, and so the word is meaningless. On other occasions, however, we may use words which seem to have concepts attached to them. In such cases, Hume argues, we should ensure that there is indeed a lineage we can trace back to experience and so establish that there really is a concept there. If we fail, we must reject the concept as empty or non-existent. In this way the empiricists' idea that all knowledge comes from experience becomes a critical tool by which to reject as unthinkable certain sorts of concept, and hence as unknowable certain areas of enquiry.

To see how this critical tool works in practice let's consider some of the philosophical problems Hume hopes to solve with it.

- What is God? To deal with this question, Hume asks where our concept of God, as a supremely powerful, infinitely wise, all-loving being, comes from. Clearly we haven't encountered God, and so it cannot come directly from him. So the concept must have come from our experiences of powerful, wise and loving people that we have encountered. Having encountered such qualities in people, we then imagine them being extended without limit. Thus, although God may have made man in his own image, the concept of God is made in man's own image according to Hume. This leaves open the possibility, radical in Hume's day, that God doesn't exist.

- Who am I? The idea of my self, Hume claims, cannot be based on any one sensation – the smell of coffee, the memory of falling off a bike, the feeling of anger – as these thoughts and emotions change constantly. So what sensations does the concept of self correspond to? Hume suggests the term 'self' is just the name for the entire series of sensation and thoughts that make up your life. It does not name a particular thing but stands for the whole bundle of conscious experiences that constitute your mind.

- What is morality? Hume points out that our concepts of good and bad cannot be traced back to any particular sensations. After all, you can't see the evil of an action, or smell the goodness of someone's character. So where do we get such concepts from? According to Hume, they come from the 'inner' sensations of our own emotions. With this discovery, Hume is able to give an extended account of the complex nature of our moral concepts as they grow out of our emotions.

Thus Hume takes on many of the big ideas in philosophy, using the simple principle of empiricism. How successful he was in each of this areas is debatable, but in the philosophical discussions of religion, the self and morality Hume is a very important figure. However, it is his treatment of the concept of causation that has led to the most discussion.

Hume on causation

more difficult

We are all aware of causes and effects. A dog's tails knocks a glass, the glass falls over. The dog has caused the water to spill. The water in turn causes the ink on the essay to run, and so on. Every minute we can witness multiple examples of causation all around us, but where does the concept come from? At first sight it seems obvious. We can see that the dog has caused the water to spill. We can see the effect of the water on the ink. We observe the one thing causing the other, and like anything else, the concept of causation derives from sensation.

However, Hume points out that things are not as simple as we thought. Using his example, consider observing one billiard ball approaching another, striking the second and the second moving off. Here it seems we have a clear case of observing one ball causing the other to move. So surely this must be the origin of our concept of causation? However, when we look more closely, it becomes clear that all we ever saw was one ball approach and come into contact with another; we heard a sound and saw the second move off; we never actually witnessed any sense datum corresponding to the cause. Imagine that all the time there were elaborate magnets under the table and that these moved the first ball up to the second, and then a separate magnet moved the second ball away, such that the first ball did not cause the second to move at all. Would this look any different? The answer must be no; but if there is no difference between the first and the second case, then we must conclude that indeed a cause is not something we actually experience in the sense data themselves, as the sense data are the same whether or not there was a cause.

So it seems that the concept of cause is not drawn from the senses. So where does it come from? Rationalists might conclude that the idea is innate. Obviously, as a good empiricist, this is not Hume's solution. An empiricist must either deny that we really have such a concept, or attempt to redefine it. Hume actually elects to do both. He claims that we tend to use the word 'cause' to link together patterns of data that frequently occur together. This is something that our minds do automatically for us. Imagine you clap your hands and a split second later you hear thunder in the distance. You would probably think nothing of it. Imagine the same thing happens again a minute later. Again, you would put it down to coincidence. But imagine the same thing happens a third, fourth, fifth and sixth time. Eventually you would begin to suppose that your clapping was causing the thunder. But this supposition cannot be based simply on the sense data involved for there is nothing different about the first clap than about the sixth. The only difference is in the repetition, the constant occurrence, of the two events. By the sixth clap your experience of the event feels very different; it now starts to feel like a causal event. Thus Hume suggests that what we mean and experience as cause and effect is really just the constant conjunction of events. The feeling of one event inevitably following the other is the result of repetition, and is little more than custom or habit. Instead of claiming that the concept of causation is meaningless, Hume suggests that it refers to the feeling of anticipation that arises in our minds when we come to expect one event to follow another, because it has done in the past.

3 Hume versus the rationalists

Hume's account of causation dealt a critical blow to traditional rationalism. If rationalism were ever to succeed, causes and effects must be necessarily connected. It must be possible to work out from a cause what effect must follow, and be able to do so by reason alone. Only then could the major laws of physics, and a general account of how the world works, be established *a priori*. The importance of necessity in rationalist thinking can be seen in Spinoza's book, *The Ethics*. At the beginning of the book he outlines his definitions and axioms from which the rest of his philosophy is derived. These definitions and axioms are thought to be so obvious and self-evident that no arguments are required to support them. One of the first axioms reads: 'From a given definite cause an effect necessarily follows.' However, as we have seen above, Hume suggests that we do not directly experience such necessity. All we experience is a constant repetition of events and this makes us feel as if one event will necessarily follow the other.

It is hard for us to imagine what life would be like without all our experiences and expectations. Just imagine we could experience life for the first time again, with our faculties intact. Hume suggests we would have no idea what effect would follow what cause, or even whether there were such things as causes and effects.

Hume

> *Adam [of Adam and Eve fame], though his rational faculties be entirely perfect, could not have inferred from the fluidity and transparency of water that it would suffocate him, or from the lights and warmth of fire that it would consume him. No object ever discovers, by the qualities which appear to the senses, either the causes which produced it, or the effects which will arise from it.[31]*

Hume suggests that no amount of reasoning would be able to work out in advance what effects would follow from which causes. There would be no contradiction in supposing that we could breathe underwater or that objects fell away from the Earth instead of towards it. It is only by experience that we come to learn how the world actually works and can then start to generalise and make theories and scientific laws about it. It is experience that makes it feel obvious or necessary that one event should follow another. If from birth every object had fallen upwards then this would feel just as natural and as necessary as objects falling down.

Hume's reasoning had a powerful legacy, particularly on another important philosopher, Immanuel Kant. Kant had been raised in the tradition of the rationalists, but upon reading Hume was also convinced that the project of rationalism – of achieving the truth through reason alone – was misguided. His masterpiece, the *Critique of Pure Reason*, sets out to show why.

Problems with empiricism

■ Can our knowledge of sense data really be the foundation of all knowledge?

Before reading on, we should recap what the empiricists are saying. If they are right, then everything that is in your mind comes ultimately from sensations and emotions. So all of your ideas and concepts are ultimately formed out of the basic units of sense. Moreover, all your beliefs about the world beyond your mind are ultimately justified in terms of acquaintance with these sense data. This must mean that you should be able to trace all your concepts back to their origin in sense experience. Simply by feeding sensations of various sorts into an empty mind, you should be able to produce a thinking being with a complex belief system like your own.

Does this strike you as a plausible claim? The eighteenth-century French philosopher Condillac (1715–80), a disciple of Locke, certainly believed so, and tried to prove it through a thought experiment. He asked his readers to imagine a statue that is organised like a human on the inside but devoid of any sensations. Perhaps you can imagine its skin is like marble and can't let any sensations in. Then imagine adding sensations to the statue's mind one by one. In his book, *A Treatise of Sensations* (1756), Condillac described the process whereby the statue is brought from having no experience at all to forming concepts and acquiring beliefs about itself and the world around it.

experimenting with ideas

1 Would Condillac's statue be able to develop all the concepts you have? Can you think of any concepts that would be beyond a being who was confined to sensation alone?
2 Could the statue develop into a being with a fully fledged belief system like your own? What problems would it face? Are there things you believe or know that such a statue could not?

■ Criticism 1: Difficulties for the empiricist account of concept formation

We've seen that traditional empiricism, like that of Locke and Condillac, claims that all our concepts are kinds of copies of sensations. My concept of the colour red is derived from my experience of it; and a more complex concept, like that of coffee, is some sort of combination of simple concepts each ultimately derived from the simple elements of sense. This may seem reasonably plausible at first sight, but once we start looking more closely at how this is supposed to work things begin to look more difficult.

To start, let's examine the simple concept of red. If my concept is a kind of copy of a sensation, which particular sensation is it a copy of? If it is a copy of one particular experience of red, then it will necessarily be a particular shade. However, my actual concept of red is not that of any specific shade. The real concept includes all shades of red. So how does the particular shade which the empiricist regards as my concept come to represent all reds? And how do I distinguish the general concept of red from the concept of the specific shade? In response to this, the empiricist might want to say that the concept must be some sort of collection of all the shades of red we have experienced; but does this idea make any sense? If colour concepts are copies of sensations, they must have a specific shade. A particular image of a colour in my mind cannot be many colours. Even if it did involve some sort of spectrum of all the reds I have so far encountered, another problem arises – namely that I wouldn't be able to recognise any new reds as red since they wouldn't be represented in my concept. The concept of coffee presents similar problems. Is it a collection of every single coffee experience I have ever had? Is it some sort of melange of all these experiences? One odd consequence of this possibility would be that I would have to have a different concept of coffee from everyone else because no two people's set of experiences are identical. So I wouldn't be talking about the same thing when discussing coffee.

Other difficulties arise when we consider that we seem able to have a concept of something without ever having experienced it. I can have the concept of coffee even if I haven't tasted it, and, similarly, I can form the concept of Spain even though I have never been there. Consider also the concept I have of an atom, something that is too small for us ever to have any sense experience of. When it comes to abstract concepts the difficulties get worse. How do I acquire the concept of justice or freedom? It seems very difficult to relate such concepts merely to patterns within experience and ultimately to patterns of sense data. After all, neither justice nor freedom looks or smells like anything; nor do they make any particular noise. In fact, they don't seem to be things that we have sense experience of at all.

An empiricist could argue that the fact that it is very difficult to explain abstract concepts in this way is why such terms are notoriously vague. They could claim that if we could pin them more closely to experience then we would have greater clarity. Here the idea has to be that we are able to form such concepts as that of justice by observing a series of just acts, but precisely how this is supposed to work remains rather unclear.

Further difficulties arise for relational concepts such as being near or far, next to or on top of. If I form the concept of a cat from seeing a cat, then how do I form the concept of the cat being on the mat. I can't actually see the 'on-ness', all that appears in sensation is the cat and the mat.

Here we have raised a host of problems for the traditional empiricist picture of how we form concepts. Since Locke's day, empiricist philosophers have grappled with these difficulties and in the process developed more sophisticated accounts of concept formation. However, we don't have room here to explore this complex area further.

■ Criticism 2: Are some ideas innate?

Rationalist philosophers often argued that certain concepts couldn't be acquired from experience. We've already looked at some of Plato's arguments for saying that mathematical concepts had to be innate: we may encounter pairs of objects in the world, but never the number two itself. He similarly argued that concepts like 'beauty' or 'justice' are not things we ever perceive in the world. We encounter beautiful things or just acts, but never beauty or justice as such. He concludes that we must acquire these concepts from somehow observing the essential nature of beauty or justice with our minds.

Descartes also argued that the concept of God, i.e. of a being perfect in every way, couldn't be acquired from experience on the grounds that nothing in experience is ever perfect. Similar problems confront the empiricist in trying to account for our concept of infinity. If everything we ever experience in this life is finite, how could experience be the source of this concept? Descartes also claimed that our concept of 'substance' could not have an empirical source.[32] Leibniz argued that we have implicit knowledge of various abstract principles – such as that nothing can be produced from nothing, or that nothing happens for no reason – that could not be discovered through experience.

Beyond philosophy, many people believe that we may have an innate moral sense, that we are somehow born knowing right from wrong. Noam Chomsky (1928–), contemporary American philosopher and political dissident, even argues that we are born with a capacity to learn language.

In another sense, it is undeniable that we are born with certain instincts and urges – to suckle, to cry, to crawl. Some (behaviourists, for example) may claim that this counts as a sort of knowledge. Certainly there is a sense in which a baby knows how to suckle, but few would want to argue that they know what they are doing or why they are inclined to do it.[33]

So it seems that there are many different ways in which we can be seen to have a sort of knowledge that is not derived from experience. How successful any of these considerations is, is a matter for discussion.

■ Criticism 3: The trap of solipsism

Another difficulty with the empiricist position is that it threatens to lead us into the trap of SOLIPSISM. To understand the difficulty we need to recall that empiricists, like Locke, follow Descartes in claiming that we perceive the physical world only indirectly. But if this is right then how do I get from the immediate knowledge I have of my own sense data to knowledge of anything beyond them, namely the physical world? If all I can be absolutely certain of is that I experience sense data, then it seems I can never be certain that anything else exists. Beliefs founded in one's own personal experience appear to be incurably subjective, and inferred beliefs about physical objects are always vulnerable to sceptical attack. Moreover, if I can't be sure that the physical world beyond my mind exists, then I cannot be sure that minds other than my own exist either. It seems that I may be completely alone! This sceptical position is known as solipsism. It is the idea that all that we can really be certain of is our own existence and experience. It could be that nothing and no one else exists.

Escaping solipsism was *the* central problematic of eighteenth-century epistemology. The credibility of both Descartes' and Locke's foundationalism hangs on whether or not it can be solved. If they are unable to escape the trap of solipsism – as many argue they are – then their epistemologies will amount to the claim that knowledge of the physical universe is impossible: a sceptical conclusion which we surely have good reason to try to avoid.[34]

■ Criticism 4: The problem of *a priori* knowledge

Another difficulty for the empiricist is to account for the special status of our knowledge of maths and logical truths. If all knowledge is gained through experience then how can we account for *a priori* truths? If I don't need to make reference to sense data to know that $2 + 3 = 5$ then we have a class of knowledge that empiricism can't explain.

The empiricist may respond by saying that all *a priori* truths are analytic; and as they tell us only about the meanings of the symbols, such truths are condemned as being able to tell us nothing of interest. Alternatively, the empiricist may answer that we do indeed gain such knowledge by experience.[35] She may claim that we observe that two apples and three apples make five apples, that two lizards and three snakes make five reptiles, and so on, and it is from such observations that we can generalise that 2 and 3 make 5. The argument is that mathematical laws are discovered in much the same way as are other laws about the world. For example, just as we see the sun rise each morning and thus generalise that it will rise every morning, or observe that delicate objects dropped from certain heights tend to break, so we observe how objects behave when grouped together and make empirical generalisations, which are the laws of addition. The difference between mathematical truths and other empirical truths is only that the evidence for them is more consistent.

However, this conclusion is not very satisfactory as it places mathematical claims on the same level as empirical generalisations and thus maths loses its status as a body of necessary truths. Not every delicate object is certain to break when dropped from a height, and eventually the sun may not rise. And even if delicate objects did always break, and the sun did always continue to rise, it is at least conceivable that this may not be the case. Yet surely 2 plus 3 will always be 5, and we just can't imagine waking up one morning and finding that they were now 6. Such an idea appears to make no sense: 2 plus 3 just has to make 5.

How might an empiricist react to such observations? One approach is to modify empiricism slightly and admit these exceptions to the general principle that all knowledge comes from experience. If we accept that reason alone is indeed the basis for mathematics and logic, we may still claim that truths of reason can never tell us anything new or interesting about the world. An empiricist may recognise that there are truths of reason, but regard them as empty of empirical content and so useless as a basis for knowledge about the physical universe. In so doing the empiricist can retain the basic point that it is only experience that can provide interesting or new information about the world. Reason's usefulness lies in unpicking implications and truths that are already present in the knowledge we have. So, for example, if I knew that Shakespeare wrote *Hamlet* and I later found out that *Hamlet* was a tragedy, I would be able to deduce, by reason alone, that Shakespeare wrote at least one tragedy. However, in doing so I would not be gaining any new knowledge but merely teasing out facts I knew implicitly already.

■ Criticism 5: Scepticism about the future and the past

You have already had occasion to consider two sceptical arguments about the possibility of knowledge of the future and of the past on page 19 and again on page 35 (scenario 2). Have a look through those sceptical scenarios once again before reading on. Both these sceptical arguments work by pointing out that knowledge of past and future has to be based on an inference. This is because neither can be observed directly – neither is an immediate part of our present sense experience. Hume's sceptical argument about INDUCTION notes that knowledge of the future is based on and inferred from knowledge given us in the past and present. Russell's argument notes that we have to infer knowledge of the past from knowledge given us in the present. Both suggest that the inferences may be unsound.

Both Russell and Hume are empiricist philosophers, and the thrust of their sceptical arguments lies in their insistence that genuine knowledge must come from immediate and present experience or from acquaintance with sense data. If one insists on this, then it is a short step for all other kinds of knowledge, knowledge inferred from sense data, to appear less than certain and even, in the final analysis, unknowable. If, to return to Condillac's statue, all it can truly know are the sense data with which it is directly acquainted, anything the statue infers from what is given to it in the present moment will be open to doubt, including knowledge of past and future. If this is right, then empiricism leads us further into scepticism and so appears inadequate as an account of how human knowledge is justified.

Modern criticisms of empiricist foundationalism

■ Criticism 6: Is knowledge of sense data really certain?

more difficult

Empiricist foundationalism suggests that our sense data, which cannot be doubted, are the building blocks for all our knowledge. However, one objection to this seeks to undermine the supposed certainty of our sense data. The critic claims that sometimes we can be unsure as to how to characterise much of our immediate experience. For example, I may see a flashy car and be unsure of whether the colour is metallic purple or magenta. Moreover I can make mistakes. I may believe that I am eating smoky bacon crisps, when in fact the crisps are paprika flavoured. But surely, the objection runs, if immediate experience is certain I could never be in such a position?

The empiricist foundationalist may feel that she has been cheated here. The obvious defence is that any uncertainty does not concern the appearance to me of the sense data. Rather the error here has to do with how I categorise or describe them. Since these are examples of possibly misdescribing what one perceives, the defence goes, they do not touch the certainty one can have of the immediate sense data themselves prior to any description. I may not be sure of what this colour or taste is called, but I can none the less be certain of what it is like here and now for me.

Another way of making the point is to say that we can avoid error so long as we resist the inclination to 'translate' the immediacy of experience into categories, or to put them into words. While we may go wrong in trying to conceptualise such experience, surely the immediacy of present sensation remains indubitable. The empiricist foundationalist maintains that this original preconceptual given is the ground for any further superstructure of ordered experience.

However, without some sort of interpretation it is difficult to see how such experience could be anything more than what the American philosopher William James (1842–1910) called a 'blooming, buzzing confusion': an undifferentiated stream of sensations. It is only by placing what is given – the stream of sense data – within certain categories that beliefs can be held as to what is the case, and any knowledge claims about it made. One would be acquainted with one's sense data, but not have any factual knowledge about them. Kant expressed the point with the well-known phrase: 'intuitions [i.e. roughly sense data] without concepts are blind'.[36] This means that sense data in themselves cannot even be experienced: the mind would be 'blind' to them because they have not yet been classified.

Whether or not we want to go so far as to say that experience of the raw, uninterpreted given is impossible, it is certainly the case that we cannot talk directly about it or say anything meaningful about what it is like. In other words, without conceptual organisation there can be no knowledge about one's own sense data. It would seem that we cannot even claim certainty for the proposition that a colour looked magenta or that the taste seemed like smoky bacon to me, here and now, since to do so is to go beyond the immediacy of the moment. This is because to describe the way something appears to you involves categorising it along with other similar experiences. Perceptual beliefs depend (if they are to be intelligible) on our being able to connect them with past experiences that are alike in a certain respect. The word 'magenta' functions to connect the present experience with many others that are not present, and to treat it as equivalent to the others in the relevant respect. In other words, the very effort to identify the immediate data of one's private experience necessarily involves going beyond what is immediate. This reference to what lies beyond the experience being described opens up any such statement to the possibility of error or misdescription. It may turn out that the present experience is not of the sort we had supposed it to be.

These considerations are supposed to establish that the possibility of error accompanies any attempt to place things within conceptual categories. Even apparently basic reports about our sense data such as 'I smell thyme' or 'I see magenta' are embedded within larger frameworks. Consequently, factual knowledge must by its very nature be open to doubt and correction and the idea that there could be an indubitable bedrock of beliefs about our own sensory states is to be rejected. Acquaintance with what is given in sense experience does not constitute any kind of factual knowledge, since factual knowledge concerns propositions about sense data, not simply those data themselves. Prior to receiving conceptual ordering or classification, the given cannot have any propositional form and so it cannot be either true or false. This means that since the given is not the kind of thing that admits of doubt, it cannot be the kind of thing that admits of certainty either, because to acquire knowledge we must run the risk of error. Therefore, it becomes meaningless to say that sense data are indubitable since only propositions about them can be doubted or not doubted. Sense data just 'are'.

■ Criticism 7: Are beliefs about our sense data incorrigible?

Finally, it has been argued that beliefs about our own sense data are not at all incorrigible. That is, they can be corrected in the light of further evidence and so cannot be self-justifying. For example, if I learn that the crisps I am eating come from a pack labelled 'paprika', I may well decide that I am mistaken in believing the taste I am experiencing to be smoky bacon. I may even start to taste the crisps differently. Here it seems I have corrected my characterisation of the original experience. Thus, contrary to the foundationalist assumptions of traditional empiricism, we can alter our beliefs about our sense data in the light of our beliefs about physical objects.

One's previous experience, and expectations, can also influence what one perceives, even though the raw sensory experience would appear to be the same. Two people looking at the same image can see different things. To take a simple example, consider this figure:

■ **Figure 3.5 *What we see depends on what we expect***

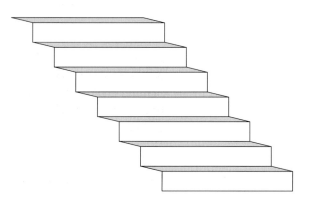

Most people see this image as a staircase going away from us, up to the left. This is doubtless because we are used to seeing staircases from this angle. But it can just as well be seen as a staircase viewed from beneath. Whichever one it happens to be, the sensory input must surely remain unchanged, so it seems that what we perceive is determined, at least in part, by what we are expecting to perceive. This implies, contrary to foundationalism, that sense data are influenced by our superstructural beliefs about the world.

Here are some other similar examples.[37] Leonardo da Vinci's drawings of the human heart show only three ventricles. How could a draughtsman of da Vinci's calibre not see the four ventricles that we now know the heart to contain? One answer is that what one sees is in large part determined by one's background assumptions. Only once people recognise the heart to be a kind of pump are they able to see four ventricles. When scientists first observed human sperm through a microscope, their background assumptions led them to observe elongated men with beards. Because they believed that sperm would have to contain small versions of the human being they would turn into, this is what they saw.

Examples like these are often taken to show that sense data propositions cannot be the foundation of empirical knowledge. Justification appears to run not exclusively from the sense data up, but in the other direction as well. Our background or superstructural beliefs are often involved in the interpretation of our sense data. If I see pink elephants floating around the room I am liable to suppose that this is a hallucination because of my background beliefs about elephants. Such a perception does not fit into my general pattern of beliefs about the world, and so it is rejected. Indeed it may be that all propositions, whether they concern sense data or not, are open to amendment in the light of other propositions, and consequently that no class of propositions, or beliefs, can be given the privileged status of being the foundations for all others.

Concluding rationalism and empiricism

We've seen how both rationalism and empiricism sought unshakeable foundations on which the rest of human knowledge could be built. Centuries later the rationalist project appears to have failed. The dream of grounding any substantial knowledge of the world on the back of the absolute certainties of reason could not be realised. Yet the rationalist attempt to start building afresh was an important step in establishing the idea that the acquisition of knowledge may require us to question received opinions, to reject traditional explanations and deploy methods of systematic and rational enquiry.

Principally through the writings of Locke and Hume, we've looked at how empiricism rejects the rationalist approach and provides its own account of the nature of the human mind and the way it forms concepts and acquires beliefs about the world. The attempt to limit the source of knowledge to sensation, however, raises its own difficulties and also leads into scepticism – for example, about knowledge of the physical world, of the past and future – and leaves doubts over whether it can provide a complete account of how our belief system is formed.

Rationalism and, to a lesser extent, empiricism have traditionally been preoccupied by the question of how we can achieve certainty. This was in part due to the importance in seventeenth-century philosophy of scepticism, but was also fuelled by the thought that without solid foundations no knowledge would be possible. Only absolute certainties could arrest the infinite regress of reasons. However, both appear to have failed to discover a suitable bedrock, suggesting that certainty about the world is unachievable. Does this mean that knowledge of the world is impossible?

While philosophers have often felt that certainty might be necessary to defeat scepticism, it is instructive to note that it is not essential to our everyday concept of knowledge. In our daily lives we claim to know all kinds of things, few of which would stand up to the arguments of philosophical scepticism. But in everyday life, we don't expect or need certainty. Is there a lesson here for the philosophers? Perhaps what is needed is a philosophical account of knowledge that does not have absolute certainty at its core: an account that reflects how we use the concept of knowledge on a daily basis.

Non-foundational accounts of knowledge

Coherentism

During our investigations into knowledge we have discovered the central importance of the notion of justification. So far, however, we have explored just one account of the structure of justification, namely foundationalism (both rationalist and empiricist varieties). The basic thought behind foundationalism is that, since it is rational to hold a belief only if it is justified or supported, our belief system as a whole must have some ultimate support or basis. Without some ground for all our beliefs, it seems we should have no good reason for believing anything. Unfortunately, however, there are various difficulties for the idea that foundational beliefs could provide the ultimate justification for all the rest. In our look at modern criticisms of empiricist foundationalism above (page 67), we questioned the supposed incorrigibility and certainty of sense data. We also argued that the direction of justification is not all one-way: that sometimes beliefs about the world can help to justify beliefs about our sense data. You may also remember in our criticisms of rationalist foundationalism that *a priori* beliefs, while they might seem absolutely certain, don't tell us anything of interest about the world. If this is right, then the idea that our body of knowledge could be structured like a building on secure foundations breaks down.

Perhaps searching for certainty at the foundation of our system of knowledge is misguided – after all, are any of our beliefs so certain that we would never give them up? In the face of new, persuasive evidence are there any beliefs that we would never be prepared to change or revise? Consider the examples below.

1 Look at the following list of beliefs. For each belief in turn, ask yourself whether it is conceivable that you could give it up. To do this, imagine a scenario which could lead you to think it false. This scenario can be as fanciful as you wish (the first example has a suggested scenario).

2 How flexible do you think your belief systems is? How much could your beliefs possibly change? Are there some beliefs that you think could never be given up?

Can you doubt that . . .

a) . . . you are having a headache? *You might go to the doctor complaining of having a headache. After examining you carefully with fancy brain-scanning equipment she patiently explains that what you thought was a headache isn't a headache at all. Apparently, the scan shows clearly that you have backache, and that people often experience such a backache as if it were a headache. Would this convince you?*

b) . . . you enjoy the taste of your raspberry pop-tart at breakfast?

c) . . . you are in love?

d) . . . mice are animals?

e) . . . you are reading this now?

f) . . . 8 × 7 is 56?

g) . . . you have a heart?

h) . . . every event has a cause?

i) . . . if Alice is taller than Thomas, and Thomas is taller than Jane, then Alice is taller than Jane?

j) . . . all sisters are female?

If there are no beliefs beyond revision, no bedrock which could bring the quest for justification to an end, then what could ever count as a good justification? If we cannot ground knowledge in absolute certainties, what makes one belief more reasonable than another? The arguments against foundationalism appear to take the ground from under our feet, exposing us to radical scepticism. Surely, we might think, there must be some ultimate grounds to secure it, otherwise genuine knowledge would be impossible.

However, according to the anti-foundationalist, this worry betrays a deep-seated prejudice that we need to escape. The error here is the foundationalist's view of justification as an all or nothing affair for which there must be some ultimate basis. But in real life justification is not like this. Some beliefs are better supported than others, but none is completely justified such that we could never come to revise it in the light of new evidence. As the philosopher of common sense also argues, the search for absolute philosophical certainty on which to ground knowledge is a vain pursuit. Such certainty can't be found, but at the same time it isn't necessary. Knowledge, justification and certainty admit of *degrees*, they are not something one either has or has not.

If we give up the quest for epistemic foundations as a lost cause and treat justification as a matter of degree, we are going to need a radically different account of the structure of knowledge. Coherentism fits the bill. According to the coherentist, the process of justification can have no ultimate ground and so the proper response to the infinite regress of justification argument is not to search for special incorrigible beliefs, but to allow that the process of justification can indeed go on indefinitely. A belief will be justified by another belief, which in turn may be justified by another. The process goes on and on, and no set of beliefs is the sole justification for the rest. In this model the justification of a belief consists of the way it fits in or *coheres* with the rest of the beliefs that one holds. The better the belief fits with one's belief system, the better justified it is.

But what exactly does it mean for a belief to 'fit in' or 'cohere' with others? One minimal thing it means is that a belief should not contradict one's other beliefs. So it would be unreasonable to believe that all cows are herbivores if one were simultaneously to believe that Daisy is a carnivorous cow. These two beliefs cannot both be true and so a rational person should reject at least one of them. In other words, they don't fit well with each other: they do not cohere.

experimenting with ideas

Which of the following beliefs cohere well with what you already believe? For each belief consider how much you would have to revise your present belief system in order to accept it.

1 When your milk teeth fall out there is a fairy who comes in the night and takes them from under your pillow, replacing them with a small sum of money in local currency.
2 When you die you leave your body and travel to a place where you meet up with other dead people.

3 Global warming is a myth and the reduction of fossil-fuel use will have no substantial beneficial effects on the environment.

4 Each of us has a soul mate who, should you be so lucky to meet, will be the love of your life.

5 The moon is made of cheese.

6 Rabbits eat mice.

7 The complexities of the human eye, the hummingbird's beak, and the delicate balance of the ecosystem are the product of design, not evolution.

8 You are the only human being. All other humanoids are replicants with no inner feelings or sensations.

9 Tony Blair is a woman.

10 Humans have never been to the moon.

But coherence entails more than simply avoiding contradictions within one's belief system. A belief is well justified not just because it doesn't contradict any other beliefs that one holds, but also because it is supported or explained by them. For example, the belief that there are four-winged, fire-breathing creatures living on a planet near Arcturus is not actively contradicted by any of my other beliefs; but it does not cohere particularly well with them either, since the rest of my beliefs give me no real reason to believe it. By contrast, my belief that the Earth is spherical is well supported – it coheres well – with all kinds of other beliefs that I hold, from those about the adventures of Columbus to trans-Atlantic air travel and astronomy. So it seems that the greater the evidential support given to a belief – the more intimately enmeshed it is with my other beliefs within the system – the better justified it is.

■ **Figure 3.6**
Foundationalism contrasted with coherentism

The foundationalist sees the structure of knowledge like a building with all our beliefs ultimately justified by secure foundations, which don't need justifying or which justify themselves. The coherentist neither agrees that such foundations can be found nor sees them as necessary. Justification, argues the coherentist, need not have any ultimate ground, it can be a matter of degree. A belief is well justified to the extent that it coheres well with the rest of one's beliefs. In the image of the web of beliefs, the nearer to the centre of the web a belief sits, the better justified it is; the further away the less well justified.

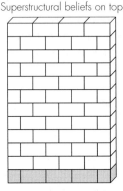

Superstructural beliefs on top

Foundational beliefs underneath

FOUNDATIONALISM

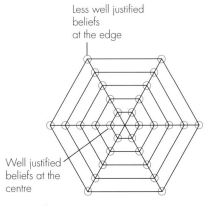

Less well justified beliefs at the edge

Well justified beliefs at the centre

COHERENTISM

To illustrate the coherentist's view of the way justification works, consider the following example. Imagine that in your youth you acquire a belief in the existence of Father Christmas. You have excellent evidence for this belief. For a start, presents always turn up under the Christmas tree on Christmas morning, and the brandy and mince pies left out for him are invariably eaten. You may even have noticed a piece of his beard caught on the fireguard, and so on. Moreover, everyone you have ever met – class mates, parents, teachers, all known to you as reliable sources of information – talk regularly and in detail about his antics. What is more, their different stories coincide on several salient points (his habit of riding a sleigh pulled by flying reindeer, his penchant for red suits and hats, and so on) in a way as to make coincidence extremely improbable.

All this is good evidence for the existence of Father Christmas. The possibility that he does not exist is not a serious contender for your assent. But there is not conclusive evidence. A sceptic might try to spoil your fun by suggesting that it could all be a part of a capitalist conspiracy to increase consumer spending. In order for it to be reasonable for you to give up your belief in Father Christmas you would have to make some fairly drastic modifications to your belief system. For example, you would have to believe that your parents were systematic liars, co-opted by big business into perpetrating a myth. You'd have to believe that everything you had seen of Father Christmas had been fabricated by them and by other adults in the community; that other children are also deceived, or also in on the conspiracy. Indeed, you would have to believe that there was a Father Christmas conspiracy of international proportions.

The coherentist's view is that at some point the competing belief that Father Christmas doesn't really exist could become a serious contender for your assent. This happens when the cost to the overall coherence of your belief system begins to be greater if you keep your belief than if you abandon it. As you grow up and your belief system expands, there comes a point when to retain a belief in Father Christmas becomes intolerable since it is inconsistent with a whole range of other beliefs that are knocking on the door for admission into the belief system. These other beliefs include: that reindeer can't fly; that whether you receive the presents you've asked Father Christmas for varies according to the financial circumstances of your parents that winter; that the world is very big and full of children and it is not possible for one man and sleigh to cover the whole area in one night. These and other considerations may eventually lead you to abandon the belief that Father Christmas exists, along with all its implications, and re-jig your belief system accordingly. This happens when the modified system is more coherent than the old.

So the new image we have of the structure of knowledge is not of a foundation of incorrigible beliefs and a superstructure, but rather of a network or web of interlocking beliefs. As we acquire new beliefs the rest of the web has to be adjusted accordingly. Those that can be accommodated only by drastic revisions to the web will generally be rejected unless such rejection would cause even greater problems of revision. Some beliefs – those at the outside of the web – are readily affected by new evidence and so can quite easily be excised. Those nearer the centre are more resistant to new evidence and will be abandoned only once it is overwhelming. So coherentism claims we are conservative about belief acquisition. We err on the side of caution, sticking with those beliefs that fit best, or cohere best with our current beliefs, and only making radical overhauls to the system when new evidence absolutely requires it.

The beliefs that coherentists generally regard as being near to the centre of the web and so most resistant to revision are *a priori* beliefs. While we should not expect such beliefs to change very often, it is significant that many coherentists do not regard them as totally beyond revision. Unlike the foundationalist, the coherentist denies that any beliefs hold such a privileged epistemic status. No beliefs are self-justifying or incorrigible. It follows that there may be extreme circumstances where such large changes have been made to our belief system as a whole that we would find it easier to give up even those beliefs which now appear self-evident.[38]

The beliefs that are generally regarded as occurring on the edges of the web are beliefs about what we perceive. These are readily updated as new perceptual evidence comes in from the environment and have less intimate links with our belief system as a whole. These perceptual beliefs feed into and must be accommodated with the web as a whole. Beliefs about these states will depend in large part on the rest of one's beliefs. For they must fit in with the system if they are to be accepted, just like any other belief. For example, my belief that I smell thyme rather than rosemary depends in part on a set of background assumptions about what has been put in the stew. If I had occasion to give up any of these background assumptions then I might be led to give up my belief about my own perceptual state. So the justification for coming to a belief about what I am perceiving isn't simply that it is given to me in some incorrigible way. Rather it depends in large part on how it fits in with my other beliefs. I come to believe I am smelling thyme because this fits best with my background beliefs.

Advantages of coherentism

One of the advantages of coherentism is that in giving up the search for absolute certainty it hopes to give us a more pragmatic and workable theory of knowledge. The project of foundationalism has failed to discover sufficient foundational or indubitable beliefs on which to ground our body of knowledge. The Cartesian approach to epistemology has left us with truths of reason, which are insufficient to give us any knowledge of the world, and an acquaintance with our own sensory states, which is also inadequate as the unique basis for developing any empirical knowledge. The search for certainty, in other words, has led us into a dead end.

But coherentism, rather than rejecting whatever is not completely certain, elects to draw upon our system of beliefs as it already exists and to operate with the tools for acquiring knowledge that are already in place. This provides us with a rationale for adopting beliefs which cohere well with our other beliefs. For example, it may be that I cannot be absolutely certain that other people have minds. They could all be elaborate robots designed by a mad scientist to deceive me. But, if I were to decide to reject the belief in other minds, my whole world would disintegrate and I would no longer be able to function properly as a social being. In other words, the belief that others have minds may not be beyond any doubt, but it coheres well with the rest of my beliefs, and at the same time helps to confer coherence upon them. It is therefore more rational for me to retain this belief until a competing belief comes along which would offer me the chance of a more coherent set of beliefs.

I may not be able to prove with absolute certainty that other people are beings who think and feel like me, but none the less, given the options, this may well be the best explanation of their behaviour. Such an explanation has considerable predictive power. For example, I may believe that people generally try to eat when they are hungry and that people get hungry when they haven't eaten for several days. I may also come to believe that Frank hasn't eaten for several days, and that he believes that there is food in the larder. Armed with these beliefs a reasonable prediction to make (all things being equal) is that Frank will try to get food out of the larder. Given that this is both a useful means of predicting Frank's behaviour and the best explanation that we have of it, in the absence of any serious competitor the coherentist can say that we are best advised to retain our belief in the existence of other minds, with all that this entails. The same will go for our belief in the existence of the physical world, and many other common-sense assumptions upon which scepticism casts doubt.

Objections to coherentism

■ 1 Some beliefs cannot be revised

► criticism ◄ An important objection to coherentism comes from those who would maintain that some beliefs are indeed incorrigible and that they cannot, therefore, ever be revised in the light of new evidence. Some beliefs are so basic, the thought goes, that they are fundamental to our belief system. We saw Descartes reason in this way when he claimed that the *cogito* was indubitable and a foundation for further knowledge. Surely, there is no way in which we could be brought to revise our belief in our own existence? He also argued that simple judgements of mathematics and *a priori* truths generally – his 'clear and distinct ideas' – could not be doubted. It is certainly difficult to conceive of the propositions of mathematics being revised.[39]

Similarly, the empiricist foundationalist might insist that knowledge of one's own sense data is so basic that it can be known immediately, irrespective of what other beliefs one holds. I can know I have a headache whether or not it fits in with any other beliefs I happen to have.

We have already seen the attraction of this traditional foundationalist way of thinking. We have also examined the arguments against it, and so it is not necessary to go over them in detail again here. When it comes to our knowledge of sense data, the coherentist will argue that it is indeed possible to doubt my own headache. If my background beliefs change, I may have to revise my judgement about what it is that I feel. Perhaps if I am shown a brain scan clearly indicating that no pain receptors are being activated I might come to change my mind about what I am experiencing. To give another example, if someone throws an ice cube down the back of my neck and tells me it's a red hot poker, I may well scream, thinking I am experiencing a burning sensation. When I discover the truth, however, I realise I was really experiencing something cold. Here changes in my background beliefs have led me to revise my judgement.

▶ criticism ◀   There is nothing in the coherentist's account of justification
to say that there can't be two or more equally justified sets of
beliefs. And so long as two sets of beliefs are equally coherent
there appears to be no way of choosing between them. Each
would have its own complex web of interlocking beliefs and
all the beliefs would be equally well justified by the way they
fit in with the rest. But since these two webs of beliefs do not
agree with each other, they cannot both be true. One web
may claim one thing about the world, which the other
contradicts. But if they can't both be true and there is no
reason to prefer one to the other, then neither can be
regarded as true and so coherentism must be false.

Another way of seeing this objection is to recognise that
coherentism regards justification exclusively as a matter of the
relations between beliefs. But this means that it ignores any
relationship between our beliefs and the way things actually
are. In other words, my beliefs could be well justified in
coherentist terms, while not accurately representing the
world, and my system of beliefs could be completely free-
floating. So in order for my system of beliefs about the world
to be properly justified it must have some basis in reality.
Empiricist foundationalists have traditionally looked to
perception to give us this basis. It is raw sense data, in other
words, which locks our belief system in with the world and
makes it *about* the world. In defence against this point, the
coherentist may point out that sense data are not beliefs and
so cannot enter into justifying relationships. For as we have
already seen, it is only something with propositional form that
can justify a belief. Sense data as such cannot justify our
beliefs about the world, since they cannot be true or false,
they simply *are*.

So what is the relationship of sense data to our beliefs about
the world? Surely there is some connection between the
sensations we experience and empirical knowledge, otherwise
there seems to be no constraint on what beliefs we have about
the world. The coherentist's answer is that it is the beliefs we
acquire about what we perceive that can enter into justifying
relations with other beliefs. The beliefs that I am perceiving a
red patch and that I am a reliable observer, amongst other
beliefs, jointly justify my belief that there is a red patch before
me. In all this, we don't jump outside of beliefs. But at the
same time beliefs about what I am perceiving don't come
from nowhere. Rather they are caused by the impact of the
world upon my sense organs. Perception, in other words, is

the *cause* of one's acquiring beliefs about the world, but not the *justification* for them. So beliefs about our perceptual states do have an important role in determining what we believe about the world, and at the same time link us in with the way the world is. (Note that this belief about the relation between the world and our sense data is one of the beliefs which helps to make the system of beliefs more coherent, and so it is one that could be given up in the light of further evidence. However, it is clearly a belief which is fairly central to the web, and so we would give it up only under extreme circumstances.)

Reliabilism

Both coherentism and foundationalism reckon that we must be able to justify our claims to know by appealing to some further beliefs which we hold. However, for many of the beliefs we hold and would want to count as knowledge, it is far from easy to say precisely what justification we have. For example, you may know all kinds of bits of so-called 'general knowledge', such as that water is H_2O, or that dolphins are mammals, or that the Battle of Hastings took place in 1066, but have no clear idea of what justification you might have for such claims. I have no idea how to demonstrate that water is composed of oxygen and hydrogen, and yet I would want to claim to know that it is. An initial response to this is to say that such knowledge is justified by the testimony of reliable authorities on these topics. It is because I have been told by some reliable source that I can claim justification for my beliefs. However, precisely where or when you first heard of these facts may also be unknown to you. In such cases, the original justification one may have had has been forgotten and so it still appears impossible for you to say exactly how the knowledge is justified. Despite this, pieces of knowledge like this do seem to be very well justified. We would be very reluctant to give them up. So it seems that there is reason to think that we have well justified beliefs even though we cannot actually say how they are justified.

In response to this one might point out that it would be fairly easy to produce a justification if required. I could go to an encyclopedia to establish any of the facts we've just mentioned. But this is not the point. We are not arguing here that one couldn't find a justification for these beliefs, but rather that we feel justified before having found any such additional justification. So the issue here is to find the evidence which is actually being used to support the belief, not the evidence which could be used. In any case, there are plenty of other examples of knowledge claims for which we have very little clue about how to justify. Many knowledge claims are unsupported by any beliefs that I currently have, or that I could conceivably acquire. For example, many beliefs about the world around us are produced by sensory inputs. This is normally a reliable method for the production of such beliefs, and so such beliefs are normally regarded as well justified. Yet, someone need have no real clue about how perception works to produce these beliefs. The mechanisms underlying perception may not be understood, and yet this seems not to disqualify it as a method of producing knowledge.

In a similar vein, consider how a farmer might select the proper time to sow a crop. We can imagine our farmer waiting for the constellation of Orion to disappear over the horizon before planting. He might have all kinds of false beliefs about why this is the correct time to plant. He might believe that once the hunter god has left the skies, this is a deliberate signal to all farmers that the hunting season should now end, and sowing begin. And yet would we want to say that he doesn't know this is the right time? Probably we would not. For although the farmer doesn't understand why – he cannot, in other words, explain why he is justified – he is none the less justified. This is because waiting for Orion to leave the skies in the northern hemisphere is indeed a reliable method for selecting the proper time to sow crops. Doing this gives the right result, as it were. Similarly, we might want to say that indigenous tribes in the Amazon rainforest know that the appearance of a certain bird means that honey is nearby, or that a certain plant cures gall stones, and yet they would have no genuine clue about how they know this or what justifies their claims.

In these cases the people in question do seem to have knowledge, even though they cannot offer any justification. This is because the justification is not something to which they have conscious access. So what makes such beliefs justified? According to reliabilism it is that the mechanism which produced the beliefs is a reliable one. The methods are ones which tend to produce true beliefs. In this view, what justifies a belief is not that it fits with or is supported by other beliefs which one explicitly has, but rather that it is acquired by a reliable method. In this sense, the justification may well be external to their mind, and yet the belief is none the less justified. A sea captain who uses a compass to navigate may have no real understanding of how a compass works, but none the less the method is a reliable one. The captain may even believe that the compass is controlled by navigating spirits, and this belief wouldn't alter the reliability of the method. So this suggests that knowledge doesn't consist in someone having any explicit understanding of the justification for their belief – all that matters is that they have reached the belief in an appropriate way. The sea captain's method is not just lucky even though it contains false beliefs. He has acquired a belief in the correct route by a reliable method although he cannot provide any justification as to why it is a justified one.

Key points: Chapter 3

What you need to know about **rationalism, empiricism and the structure of knowledge**:

1 *A priori* knowledge can be acquired prior to, or independently of, experience. By contrast, *a posteriori* or empirical knowledge depends upon evidence that can be gained only through experience.

2 Analytic propositions are those which are true by definition and cannot be denied without contradiction. Synthetic propositions cannot be known simply by analysis of the meanings of the terms in which they are expressed and so can only be seen to be true *a posteriori*.

3 Rationalism is the view that reason, as opposed to sense experience, is the primary source of the knowledge of which we are capable. Rationalists are impressed by the certainty and immutability of mathematical knowledge and try to establish knowledge in other areas, such as in ethics or the physical sciences, with the same degree of certainty by reasoning purely *a priori*.

4 However, the rationalist project faces the difficulty that truths discoverable by reason alone appear to tell us nothing about the way the world is. Hume argued that knowledge of the physical universe requires empirical investigation.

5 Empiricism looks to experience rather than reason as the source of our concepts and the foundations for all beliefs about the world. Concepts are formed as copies of sensations. Knowledge of the world is justified in terms of the immediate and incorrigible data of sense.

6 One important difficulty for empiricism is that it can lead into solipsism. If all our concepts come from our own sense experience, it may seem that we cannot acquire knowledge of the physical world beyond that experience.

7 Coherentisim is an alternative account to foundationalism of the structure of knowledge. It claims that no beliefs are basic and therefore that all beliefs need justification in terms of further beliefs. By this account, beliefs are more or less well justified to the extent that they fit in or cohere with other beliefs in the system.

8 Reliabilism is the view of justification which claims that a belief is justified if it is produced by a reliable method rather than by being based on good reasons. A reliable method is one which is most likely to produce a true belief.

Knowledge and perception

Introduction

How do we acquire knowledge of the world? An obvious answer is that we learn about it through our senses. We know that the cat is on the mat because we can *see* it there. We know that it is a hot day because we can *feel* the warmth of the sun on our backs. However, we have already had occasion to raise doubts about the reliability of our senses in telling us about the world. So just how accurate are the human sense organs as indicators of the way the world really is? It is interesting to observe in this connection that other animals have senses that are far more sensitive than our own. Dogs, for example, can hear sounds that are too high for us to hear, and they can smell all kinds of things that we can't. Does this mean they are perceiving the world more accurately than us? Other creatures have senses completely different from ours. The ability of sharks to sense the electric field created by living things, or of bats to use sound to navigate, raises the question of what the world must seem like to these animals. How do their senses represent the world in their minds? In colours and shapes? In textures and sounds? Or in some way we simply cannot imagine? Perhaps these animals have a truer perception of the world than we do. Or perhaps no animal sees the world as it truly is.

experimenting with ideas

1 a) Do you think your favourite food tastes the same to a dog as it does to you?
   b) Do you think dog food tastes the same to you as to a dog?
   c) Who has a truer perception of the world: dogs or humans?
2 Some creatures lack the senses we have. They may be blind or deaf. Others have senses that we don't have. They may detect electricity or magnetic fields. How many senses must a creature have for it to get a true picture of the world? Give a list of the necessary senses.
3 Dogs can hear high frequency sound waves that we do not register. Likewise, elephants hear frequencies lower than we can register. Does it follow that all humans are partially deaf? Are some sounds so low and others so high that no creature can hear them?

4 As with sound waves we only perceive light waves within a particular bandwidth. Imagine meeting an alien who does not perceive the frequencies of light that we do, but perceives a whole set of higher ones such as ultra violet and beyond. The alien represents these waves in a range of colours much as we do. Who sees the true colours of the world: humans or aliens? If neither of us does, does that mean that no colours are the real colours?

5 Can you be sure that, when you and your friend share a piece of chicken, the flavour you experience is actually the same for both of you? Similarly, is there any way of telling that you are seeing exactly the same colours as someone else?

6 Sound is caused by compression waves of air hitting your ear drum. If a tree fell down in a forest and there were no ears around (human or otherwise), would it:

  a) make a sound?

  b) just produce airwaves?

7 Where are rainbows? Are they in the sky, in rain droplets, in people's minds or nowhere?

These questions raise all sorts of puzzles about how perception works and what it can tell us about the world. What should be evident from having considered them is that we need to be clear about what is going on in perception before we can be completely confident about our answers. In other words, we need to develop some kind of theory of perception. In this chapter we will consider some of the main philosophical theories of perception. The chapter is divided as follows:

- Realism and anti-realism
- Realist theories of perception
- Anti-realist theories of perception
- Conclusion
- Key points you need to know about knowledge and perception.

Realism and anti-realism

Much of the debate on perception hinges on the question of how much of what we perceive is really a feature of the world and how much is a feature of our minds. In other words, how much of what we are perceiving is really out there? This question of what is real or not is also central to many other areas of philosophy. If you are a REALIST about something, then you believe it exists independently of our minds. If you are an ANTI-REALIST about something, you think it is mind-dependent. The exercises opposite reveal on which topics you are a realist and on which you take an anti-realist stance.

experimenting with ideas

For each of the following, consider whether the object or topic in question is real or not. For this exercise, take 'real' to mean 'has an existence independent of minds – human or otherwise'.

	Real	Not real	Don't know
1 Numbers, e.g. the number 7	☐	☐	☐
2 Your reflection in the mirror	☐	☐	☐
3 Colours, e.g. red	☐	☐	☐
4 Smells	☐	☐	☐
5 Morality	☐	☐	☐
6 Electrons	☐	☐	☐
7 Scientific laws, e.g. $e=mc^2$	☐	☐	☐
8 Ghosts	☐	☐	☐
9 Matter	☐	☐	☐
10 Beauty	☐	☐	☐

■ Real or not?

1 Numbers, e.g. the number 7
Whether numbers are real or not has vexed many a philosopher and is still a current debate. Plato famously thought that numbers existed independently of humans, not in the world that we see and touch, but in a world we can only perceive with our minds; a world of ideas or 'forms'. He in turn was greatly influenced by another Ancient Greek philosopher, Pythagoras, who thought that to understand the world truly one must look for the mathematical structures that lie behind appearances. Pythagoras sought to uncover these structures and, amongst other things, revealed how music and harmony have a mathematical basis.

2 Your reflection in the mirror
Is your reflection behind the mirror, in your mind or nowhere?

3 Colours, e.g. red
Some will argue that the word 'red' refers to the way humans see a particular wavelength of light when it hits their retinas. Others see it as the name for the particular wavelength itself. It could also be the name for a physical object's propensity to bounce back visible light at a particular frequency. So red could be in the head, in the air or on the tomato.

4 Morality

Are good and evil objectively real? This is a key question in moral philosophy. Those who think that morality exists independently of human minds, perhaps as a creation of God or as an objecive moral law, are realists. Those who think that morality is in some sense a product of human minds are anti-realists.

5 Beauty

Some may argue that the concept of beauty – whether in the setting of the sun or the song of the nightingale – is so universal that there must be an external standard of beauty to which these things refer. Others think that beauty is subjective – or at most culturally ingrained – and is thus solely in the eye of the beholder.

6 Electrons

Some take the view that electrons and other such entities that cannot be directly observed are just a useful story we invent to make sense of experimental data. Others believe that such objects do exist and exist as we conceive them.

7 Scientific laws, e.g. e=mc^2

Scientific laws are undoubtedly formulated in the minds of humans, but to be successful they must be able to explain and predict aspects of the world. This raises the question of how real they are and whether there is something out there to which the law could correspond. Some anti-realists take the view that the laws do not correspond to anything and cannot really be said to be true or false. Instead, they are merely instrumental in helping humans control and manipulate the world. A realist may take the view that scientific laws, as they slowly evolve, edge ever closer to the truth – that is, to matching the laws of the universe.

8 Matter

Some argue that the only thing of which we are ever aware are ideas or sensations in our minds and that matter is just a convenient way of talking about these sensations. Most people believe that there is a material universe that we perceive all around us.

Realist theories of perception

Naïve (or direct) realism

The DIRECT REALIST theory of perception is the kind of view people tend to have before they have thought much about the issues. It is, in other words, the position of common sense. For this reason it is often, and rather unfairly, termed NAÏVE REALISM, despite the fact that it can be supported by sophisticated philosophical arguments. So let's outline its main theses.

Naïve realism claims that the world is pretty much as it appears to our senses. All objects are composed of matter; they occupy space, and have properties such as size, shape, texture, smell, taste and colour. These properties are perceived directly. In other words, when we look at and touch things we see and feel those things themselves and so perceive them as they really are. Objects continue to observe the laws of physics and retain their properties whether or not there is anyone present to observe them doing so. So, when we leave the room the objects in it remain and retain all the properties we perceive them to have. If a tree falls in a forest it makes a noise whether or not there is anyone there to hear it.

■ **Figure 4.1 Naïve realism**

The common-sense view of perception says that we see, hear and smell things directly as they are. Our sense organs detect properties of objects which exist out there in the world, and all of us perceive the same objects with the same properties.

Someone's sense organs

Physical object

Someone else's sense organs

In sum, the naïve realist is saying that we perceive objects with certain properties because they are there and have those properties, and we know they are there and have the properties they do because we perceive them.

Criticisms of naïve realism

Most philosophers have felt that naïve realism cannot be maintained. David Hume, for example, claimed that once one had engaged in 'the slightest philosophy'[40] one would be forced to give it up.

▶ criticism ◀ To take one immediate problem, consider perspective. As objects move away from us they appear much smaller. Likewise the gap between railway lines seems to narrow as we gaze into the distance. However, we know that objects do not actually get smaller as they get further away and we know, by travelling beside a track, that the gap between the lines remains the same. So straight away we can conclude that the world cannot be exactly as it appears to us, for it appears that objects get smaller when, in fact, they do not. To avoid having to construct some strange theory about how objects actually shrink as they move further away, it seems that the out-and-out realist must concede defeat. Objects cannot be exactly as we perceive them to be.

▶ criticism ◀ There are further and related difficulties that direct realism faces, many of which were highlighted by the second of the great British empiricist philosophers, George Berkeley (1685–1753) in one of his *Three Dialogues between Hylas and Philonous* (1713). The character of Philonous, Berkeley's spokesman, asks Hylas to consider what the colour of some distant clouds is.

Philonous:	*Let me know, whether the same colours which we see, exist in external bodies, or some other.*
Hylas:	*The very same.*
Philonous:	*What! Are then the beautiful red and purple we see on yonder clouds, really in them? Or do you imagine they have in themselves any other form than that of a dark mist or vapour?*
Hylas:	*I must own, Philonous, those colours are not really in the clouds as they seem to be at this distance. They are only apparent colours.*
Philonous:	*Apparent call you them? How shall we distinguish these apparent colours from real?*
Hylas:	*Very easily. Those are to be thought apparent which, appearing only at a distance, vanish upon a nearer approach.*
Philonous:	*And those I suppose are to be thought real which are discovered by the most near and exact survey.*
Hylas:	*Right.*
Philonous:	*Is the nearest and exactest survey made by the help of a microscope, or by the naked eye?*

Hylas: *By a microscope doubtless.*

Philonous: *But a microscope often discovers colours in an object different from those perceived by the unassisted sight. And in case we had microscopes magnifying to any assigned degree; it is certain, that no object whatsoever viewed through them, would appear in the same colour which it exhibits to the naked eye.*

Hylas: *And what will you conclude from all this? You cannot argue that there are really and naturally no colours on objects; because by artificial managements they may be altered, or made to vanish.*

Philonous: *I think it may evidently be concluded from your own concessions, that all the colours we see with our naked eyes, are only apparent as those on the clouds, since they vanish upon a more close and accurate inspection, which is afforded us by a microscope.*[41]

Since the clouds may appear red from a distance, and any number of colours from different perspectives, according to Berkeley it makes no sense to suppose that they have any *real* colour. This goes just as well for any objects. If we look closely at a flower through a microscope its colour will be different from how it looks with the naked eye. So we are forced to say that the colour is merely an effect made upon us by physical things, and not something in the objects themselves. In other words, colour is an appearance to us, not something objectively real.

■ **Figure 4.2
Berkeley's example
of observing clouds**

The clouds appear different colours to different observers. But who is right? No one has any privileged perspective, and so no one can observe the true colour. Therefore colour is an appearance to observers, and not something real.

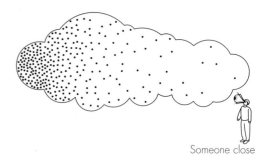

Someone close

Someone far off

Another of Berkeley's examples is that of putting a hot hand and a cold hand into the same bucket of lukewarm water. The water then feels cold to one hand and hot to the other. But clearly the same small area of water cannot really be both hot and cold at the same time. This would be a contradiction. So the conclusion follows that it must merely appear to be hot and cold. Heat and cold, therefore, are not real properties of objects but effects such objects have on observers like us.[42]

▶ criticism ◀ Another problem with naïve realism is that the justification for the theory appears circular. To see this consider how the sceptical philosopher might question the naïve realist:

Sceptic:	*So how do we know what the world around us is really like? Couldn't it be very different from the way it seems to us?*
Naïve realist:	*Don't be silly. Our senses reveal the world directly to us. They enable us to perceive the world with all its properties. So what you perceive is what there is.*
Sceptic:	*But how can you be sure that we perceive it as it really is? It could be that the senses distort the world and that objects don't really have the properties they seem to.*
Naïve realist:	*But we can tell that objects have various properties, colours, smells, tastes and so on, because we can perceive them. If they weren't there we wouldn't be able to see them, would we? So we perceive what we perceive because it is there, and so obviously we see things as they really are.*

The problem here is that the naïve realist's claim that we know what physical objects are like by perceiving them relies on the claim that we perceive things as they are. However, the claim that we perceive things as they are presupposes that we know what they are like. So the naïve realist is arguing in a circle.

An obvious response to this complaint is for the naïve realist to say that we can know that what we are perceiving really is there by appealing to the testimony of other people. If someone else is able to perceive the object in question and agrees that it has the relevant properties, then that should establish that my perception is accurate. So if I see a banana as yellow, and you see it as yellow, then one would think that it must be yellow. However, the sceptic may not be impressed by such a line of defence. The difficulty is that the perception of the second observer is plagued by the same difficulty as mine. If the human perceptual system distorts reality, then it will distort it in the same way for all humans. The fact that we both see a banana as yellow tells us about the way we see bananas, rather than the way bananas are. Using another human doesn't get round the question of whether humans perceive things as they are.

▶ criticism ◀ Also, using the testimony of others does not really help, for we know that some people perceive the world differently, perhaps because of colour-blindness, so the world cannot be exactly how it appears to everyone. We ourselves also perceive the world differently at different times. A red object may change in tone as the light changes; an object may appear smaller than it really is if observed at a distance. If the naïve realist concedes that the 'real' colour or size is different from how it appears, she will have to drop her claim always to perceive things directly as they are.

Furthermore, we are on occasion subject to illusions and hallucinations. Such deceptive perceptions show not just that we don't always see things as they truly are but, worse, that we can even seem to see things that are not there. The problem for the naïve realist is that if the world is exactly as it appears then hallucinations and illusion must, contrary to popular belief, actually be a part of the world. The naïve realist cannot seem to distinguish perceiving something which is there, and seeming to perceive something which in reality is not there.

Primary and secondary qualities

Many of the arguments against naïve realism hinge on the idea that some of the properties we perceive, such as colours, tastes and smells, are not actually properties of the objects themselves. The objects may indeed possess certain properties such as size and shape but other properties such as colour and taste appear to be more subjective and seem to rely on a mind being present. To understand this point, it may be instructive to consider the property of value. Does a one pound coin actually have that property? Could an alien place the coin under the microscope and discern that it has the property of value? 'No' is the obvious answer. The alien would be able to tell its size, the metals from which it is composed and its density but would not be able to measure its value. Value does not actually inhere in the object itself but is caused by the role the object plays in a human society. So while we talk of the coin having a value, its value is not strictly a real property of the coin at all.

The same can be said for other supposed properties of the coin. Consider its colour. Imagine the alien has no colour vision at all, but only perceives light in black and white. Better still, imagine the alien has no eyes at all but has senses that we lack, such as sonic vision and electro-sense. The alien would measure the pound coin, would know all of its physical properties and would know how it absorbs and emits light waves. But the alien would not know how humans perceive this coin as golden-coloured as it would not know how humans perceive the various wavelengths of light. So even if the alien produced a complete physical description of the coin it would not include the colour of the coin, only the wavelength of light the coin bounces back. Yet the alien's description would not be lacking in any important way, so it seems we must conclude that the coin does not have the property of being coloured in the same way that it has other properties such as shape and density.

Now consider smell. Current science suggests that smell is actually caused by the shapes of molecules. On the inside of our noses are thousands of receptors of different shapes and sizes. When we inhale, millions of molecules whizz up through our noses and, if they are the right shape and size, some of these molecules will lodge briefly in these receptors. If enough molecules of the same type do this then we perceive a smell. So the smell really represents the shape of a molecule. Molecules are not coated with a smelly property that we somehow perceive. They merely have a shape which, in humans, causes the subjective experience of a smell.

Thus it would seem that objects physically possess some properties, whereas other properties are related to the minds experiencing them. The technical terms for the real properties of objects and the somehow less 'real' properties are PRIMARY AND SECONDARY QUALITIES respectively.

ACTIVITY

Here are some possible properties of things. Which of these properties do you think are primary – properties that actually belong to objects? Which are secondary – in some sense reliant on humans or minds?

	Primary: property of object	Secondary: combination of object and mind
Mass	☐	☐
Fun	☐	☐
Yellow	☐	☐
Bitterness	☐	☐
10 metres wide	☐	☐
Density	☐	☐
Smell	☐	☐
Motion	☐	☐
Roughness	☐	☐
Circular	☐	☐
Vibration	☐	☐
Dangerous	☐	☐
Loud	☐	☐
Sweet-smelling	☐	☐
Importance	☐	☐

■ **Figure 4.3 *Where is the green of the tree?***

The word 'green' appears to have various meanings. It can refer to something in the leaves themselves: the objective property that the naïve realist says they have. It can refer to the power the leaves have to absorb and emit various wavelengths of light. It can refer to the specific wavelength itself that leaves typically emit. Or it can refer to the experience of the colour as it appears to us in our minds.

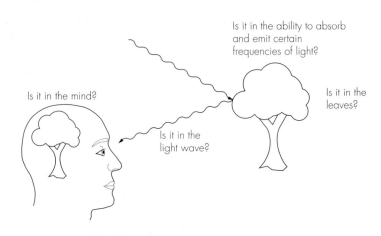

Is it in the ability to absorb and emit certain frequencies of light?

Is it in the mind?

Is it in the leaves?

Is it in the light wave?

Primary and secondary qualtties are not always defined or divided up in precisely the same way by philosophers. But a traditional division is set out in the table below. Did you agree? How would you place these various qualities?

Primary qualities i.e. real, physical qualities of the object	Secondary qualities i.e. the 'powers' of the object that produce experiences in humans (and other animals)	Other associated properties, often a social concept but in part result of the primary or secondary qualities
Position (i.e. where the object is) Number (i.e. how many there are) Shape Size (i.e. how big it is) Motion (i.e. how fast it is moving)	Colour Heat and cold Smell Sound Taste	Beauty Value Addictive Importance Disposable

People often find it difficult to recall which are the primary and which the secondary qualities. One way to think about the difference and so remember the terminology is to regard the primary qualities as those that are in objects from the *beginning* or *primarily*, that is before anyone comes along to perceive them. By contrast, the secondary qualities are those which appear only *secondarily*, when minds arrive on the scene to perceive things. In a world without perceivers there would be lots of objects with primary qualities reacting to each other; they would collide, melt, dissolve and so forth. The objects in this world can also be said to have secondary qualities as they would still have the potential to produce subjective experiences in perceivers should any appear. But without the perceivers there would be no experiences of the secondary qualities and no sensations of colour, sound or smell.

Another way of conceiving the difference between primary and secondary qualities is to consider how physical objects behave. Physical objects act and interact with one another purely on the basis of their primary qualities. The outcome of a collision between two moving objects, say billiard balls, depends on their mass, direction of movement, speed, and how they are held together by the atoms that compose them. In other words, the outcome depends entirely on the primary qualities of the objects involved. Secondary qualities have nothing to do with how objects behave. Secondary qualities are just the powers of an object to produce experiences in perceivers. This cannot have an effect on how physical objects interact with each other.

Also, note that secondary qualities ultimately boil down to primary qualities. Consider the example of smell given above. A smell is a secondary quality – a power of a molecule to produce a subjective experience in a perceiver. However, a molecule has this power in virtue of the organisation of its parts and this organisation is a matter of the primary qualities (shape, size and so on) alone. So although objects can be said to have secondary qualities, in terms of physics alone they have only primary qualities. These primary qualities have the potential to cause specific experiences in humans, and it is this potential we term a secondary quality. Thus it can be said that a secondary quality is simply the potential of a primary quality to produce an experience in a perceiver.

Other than the argument offered by Berkeley, which we have discussed, there are other considerations which have led philosophers to draw the primary/secondary quality distinction. (Note that Berkeley himself does not subscribe to this distinction.)

1 All the primary qualities lend themselves readily to mathematical or geometric description. They are readily *measurable*. The positions of any objects relative to any others can be precisely described, as can their number, shape, speed and so forth. So I can say that one object is moving three times as fast as another, that it is twice as big and so on. And I can meaningfully say that a hexagon has twice the number of sides as a triangle. However, subjectively experienced smells, colours and so on just don't behave like this. Cheese and onion flavour could never be twice salt and vinegar or any other flavour. I can't subtract the smell of lavender from that of thyme. I can't weigh the taste of coffee, or calculate the inertia of the smell of bacon. We can't add, subtract, divide or multiply tastes, flavours, colours, touches, or smells in the same way that we can sizes, shapes, speeds, masses and quantities. So it seems that secondary qualities are less amenable to being represented mathematically.

If you have studied Descartes' *Meditations* you will notice his making much of this way of thinking about the physical world in drawing his own primary/secondary quality distinction in *Meditation 6*. However, for him, only those qualities that can be represented geometrically are real and this leads him to exclude weight and hardness which have no shape, position or size. Locke draws the distinction slightly differently and includes these two in the list of primary qualities.[43]

2 The discoveries of the natural sciences may also lead us to suppose that the world cannot be precisely as it appears to be. For example, physics tells us that light is a form of electro-magnetic radiation and that what we perceive as different colours are in reality simply light waves of different lengths. Light in itself, in other words, is not coloured. In reality it possesses only the primary qualities of having a certain magnitude of wavelength, of travelling at a particular speed, and so on. Similarly, heat in objects cannot properly be said to be hot or cold. Rather our experience of hot and cold is produced by our coming into contact with physical objects with differing mean kinetic energy levels among their component atoms and molecules. The sounds we experience are also not things with independent existences. Rather they are produced in us by compression waves of air impacting on our eardrums.

3 Some philosophers have argued that certain properties are essential to objects while others are not. They have then used this distinction to argue that the essential ones must be primary, while the inessential ones are secondary. There are different ways of distinguishing the essential from the inessential properties of an object. One method involves simply working out which ones we can and cannot conceive of an object's lacking. Inessential properties are those that you can imagine an object without, while it remains the object in question. Essential properties are those you cannot imagine the thing without, while it remains the same thing.

To illustrate this point, consider the following thought experiment about a bachelor. Can you imagine a bachelor who is hungry? Would he still be a bachelor if he were bald? Clearly yes. So being well fed and having a full head of hair are not essential properties of a bachelor. However, would a man still be a bachelor if he got married? Clearly not. You can't be a married bachelor. Such a thing is inconceivable. Would he still be a bachelor if he had a sex change? No. You can't be a bachelor unless you are male. So being unmarried and being male are essential properties of being a bachelor.[44]

Now let's apply this same method to physical objects and their properties. Think of an object, say an apple. If you imagine it is making no sound (which is not difficult to do) then you are still thinking of an object (a silent apple). So making a noise cannot be an essential property of an object like an apple. Similarly, if you suppose it to have no odour, then you are still thinking of an object. Next subtract its flavour. Still you are thinking of an object, albeit not a very appetising one. You may say that it is no longer an apple, but certainly it is still an object of some sort. But now let's go further and imagine it without any colour. Again, it is plausible to argue that you are still thinking of an object, only now it is invisible. Perhaps it has been 'cloaked' by some alien technology that bends the light waves around its surface so that our eyes cannot detect it. So here we have subtracted sound, odour, flavour and colour but we are still thinking of an object. This suggests that these qualities are inessential and so that it is possible for an object to exist without them. Many objects would appear to fall into this category such as certain gases (at least when motionless), bacteria, and perhaps ghosts.

But let us return to our apple and imagine it devoid of any shape, size, position or motion, either still or moving. Here, it seems our imagination fails us. An object cannot lack these properties and remain an object. An object cannot be neither moving nor still. It cannot be completely without shape. It must have a particular size and occupy a specific position in space. It would seem, then, that these properties are not properties an object could lack in reality. If they are essential to the object they cannot be properties that we merely perceive in it, but which aren't really there. It follows that they must be primary qualities. At the same time, those qualities that we can imagine an object doing without must be inessential, and so plausibly they exist only through their relations with perceiving beings like ourselves.

So there are many reasons to suggest that we should hold some sort of primary/secondary quality distinction, and it appears we must make a distinction between how the world appears to us and how it really is. But if the world is not exactly as it appears, then we can no longer hold onto a naïve realist position. We must therefore look to another theory to explain what is going on when we perceive the world.

Representative realism

Having done the 'slightest philosophy' we can no longer hold onto the idea that we perceive things directly as they are. Having recognised a distinction between appearance and reality, the natural next step is towards a REPRESENTATIVE REALIST theory of perception (or INDIRECT REALISM). The representative realist agrees with the naïve realist that the world consists of material objects which occupy a public space and that these material objects possess certain independently existing properties. This commitment to the real existence of matter with real properties is what makes them both realists. However, the representative realist disagrees with her naïve realist counterpart over whether we perceive the properties of matter directly and as they are. She distinguishes our sensations or sense data from the *objects perceived*. In other words, the claim is that there is, on the one hand, a mental component – namely the way the object appears to the observer – and, on the other, the object as it is in reality. For the representative realist, sensations are a REPRESENTATION or image of the world. It's as if we had pictures in our minds which represent to us the real world outside of our minds.

■ Figure 4.4
Representative realism

Representative realism distinguishes our sensations or sense data from the thing perceived. The physical object causes a sensation in us which is a representation of the real thing. So we now have two worlds: the world as it is in itself, and a picture of the world as it appears to our minds. But how accurate is our representation of the world? According to representative realism, some aspects of our sensations are accurate while others are not. So, our representation of the so-called primary qualities of size, shape, position, and motion represent accurately what is out there. Physical objects really have these properties. But our experiences of colour, sound, smell, taste and so on, do not. These properties do not exist in the objects themselves in the same way that primary qualities do. Rather such sensations are imperfect representations produced in us by the secondary qualities of objects. So our different experiences of smells represent different shapes of molecules, for example.

Perceived object   Real object

By using this distinction the representative realist hopes to explain sense deception. Deception occurs when the sense data do not match up with the object. When the image I have in my mind, for whatever reason, does not accurately correspond to the way things are in the world, I am subject to some sort of illusion. It can also explain how hallucinations are possible. They occur when a sensation occurs in the mind but there is nothing corresponding to it in the world.

The representative realist also explains the difference between primary and secondary qualities. Some of those properties that we perceive to be in objects really are there, and some are not. So the former are accurate reflections of the way the world is in reality, and should form the basis for our knowledge of the world, while the latter are untrustworthy illusions.[45] However, this is not to say that our sensations of colour, sound, smell and so on are completely misleading, since they do map onto real differences in the objects but at a scale too small for us to detect. As Locke explains, the primary qualities are 'utterly inseparable from [. . .] body' while secondary qualities are 'nothing in objects themselves, but powers to produce various sensations in us'.[46] So, for example, colour, a sensation in the mind, represents certain secondary qualities the surface of an object has, namely its ability to absorb, emit and reflect light. In other words, the wavelengths of light get 'translated' or interpreted by us into our experience of colour. Similarly, smell represents the shape of a molecule: our nose and brain somehow translate the molecule into the smell. So the molecule itself isn't smelly. This is just an effect the molecule makes on us. In this way, the real world of primary qualities is represented to us as a world of colour, smells, tastes and so on.

One way to understand what the representative realist is saying is to imagine yourself reduced to the size of a molecule of air with some special ship in which to get around the world. Imagine observing what happens when a person smells a smell, hears a sound or sees a colour. Nothing in what you observe would be smelly, noisy or colourful. The molecules producing the smell wouldn't themselves smell, nor would the compression waves of air you observe have any sound. The wavelengths of light entering someone's eyes would have a particular length, but no colour; and neither would the surfaces of the things that reflect these wavelengths. (How precisely one would observe the real world if so reduced in size is a difficulty we will ignore.) So, in this account, the real world is odourless, colourless and silent: a world describable only in the language of matter in motion. However, you would be able to see how the arrangements of the normally invisible parts which compose physical objects produce certain reactions in human sense organs. The powers to produce these reactions are the secondary qualities.

Representative realism is the preferred view of most modern philosophers since Descartes, including Descartes himself and Locke. Locke distinguished between internal, private sensations (sense data) and external, publicly observable physical objects. We can only come to know about the latter through observation of the former, and so long as we know when and which aspects of our sense data are accurate representations of the external world we can use our senses to build up an accurate picture of it. Representative realism also fits in very well with the current scientific view of the world. As we saw above, scientists these days tell us that colours, smells, sounds and so forth don't exist in the world as it is in itself. What really exists are light waves, chemicals and compression waves of air, all of which can be described in geometric and mathematical terms.

Finally, note that representative realism helps us to understand the well-known philosophical question: whether a tree, when it falls down in a forest when there is no one there to hear it, makes a noise. The answer is yes and no! Yes, in as much as the noise is a secondary quality, i.e. a power to produce an experience in humans. But no, in the sense that if there were no perceivers then there would be no subjective experience of a noise, but only compression waves of air. The same must also go for the colours, smells and tastes of the tree.

Criticisms of representative realism

However, as one might have expected, difficulties arise. Representative realism has set up a sort of two-world view to explain perception. There is world number one – the world as it really is. Here, objects with primary qualities happily obey the laws of physics in their colourless, soundless, tasteless and odour-free world. It is this world, in conjunction with our human brains, that causes us to perceive world number two – the colourful, smelly, tasty world we see around us. Of course, these two worlds are not really separate: world number two, the world we perceive, is simply a representation of world number one, the world as it is.

▶ criticism ◀ Once this two-world account of perception has been established, serious philosophical problems arise. One crucial difficulty concerns how we are to tell when our senses are and are not deceiving us. If what we perceive is a kind of representation of the world, how do we know how accurate that representation is? In other words, how can we be sure that the world we perceive (world two) in any way resembles the world as it is (world one)? Critics of representative realism would claim that we can only ever perceive secondary qualities, we never perceive primary qualities directly. Everything we perceive must come from our five senses and these produce all the colours, sounds, tastes, smells and touches that make up the secondary qualities. So we have to infer the existence of an independent object with primary qualities purely from our awareness of secondary qualities. In this sense, our idea of a primary world of just shapes, sizes, masses and motions must be a sort of abstraction from the secondary qualities we perceive. But if the existence of physical objects is just inferred from our senses, how can we be sure that our senses are accurate in their representation? Without independent access we cannot place our sensations and the physical objects side by side in order to make a comparison. In other words, we can't get out of our own minds and adopt a God's-eye view, as it were, from which to observe both our sense data and the world. But without such a point of view we cannot establish when we are being deceived or how accurate our representations are.

Another way to see this point is to imagine that you were born and raised inside a cinema. Suppose that you spent all your days watching movies, but were never allowed to leave to visit the outside world. Living such a restricted life you would doubtless have dreams of escaping. You would wonder what it was like beyond the walls of your prison. But imagine what a distorted picture you would have of life outside the cinema. Given that all you had to go on would be the films you had seen you would doubtless fantasise about meeting the likes of Indiana Jones and Buzz Lightyear. Because you could never compare reality with the movies, you would be in no position to judge what was fact and what was fiction.

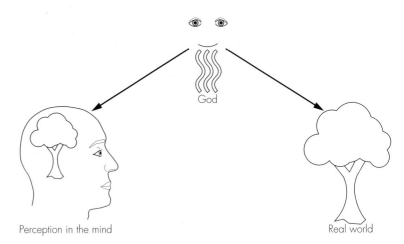

■ **Figure 4.5**
Representative realism faces a problem

To determine how accurate our perception of the world is, we would have to compare our representations of it in our minds with the world as it is in itself. But to do this we would need to get out of our own mind and adopt a 'God's-eye' point of view. This, of course, is impossible.

Perception in the mind

God

Real world

▶ criticism ◀ In separating the world as it appears from the world as it really is, representative realism has made this latter world seemingly inaccessible to our senses. The two-world account of perception has created a gap between the world as it appears and the world as it really is, and this gap seems to be an insurmountable chasm. A *veil of perception* has dropped down between us and the world, meaning that we only ever have access to our representations and cannot peer beyond the veil to see the world as it really is.

So it appears we cannot know whether the world we perceive is an accurate representation of the world as it really is. The real world could be radically different from the way it appears to us and, because we can't penetrate the veil, we will never be able to know what it is really like. One line of defence against this objection is that if the world we perceive did not, in important ways, match the world as it really is, then we would not survive. We would have been unable to hunt and catch animals, or find the nuts and berries needed to nourish and sustain ourselves, and would have died out long ago. We have survived, so our representation of the world must be fairly accurate. Our senses have evolved precisely to give us an accurate representation of the world as it is, so the relationship between the two worlds must be sound.

This defence may well satisfy some. It suggests that our representations are correlated systematically with the world and so seems to provide some assurance that they represent something real. However, it still doesn't tell us how accurate our perception is. It could well be that our senses are rigged up to help us survive in the world, but that in the process they distort it completely. There is no guarantee that the best way of ensuring a species' survival is for it to evolve an accurate perception of its environment. The way it is useful to perceive things need not be a good indication of the way things are.

But there are worse problems for this line of defence. Recall how in Chapter 2 the sceptic raised powerful doubts about the nature of the external world, claiming that our present sensations could be caused by something entirely different – a dream, a powerful demon, a virtual reality machine or by being a brain in a vat. Now, even if these possibilities are far-fetched, the very fact that they are conceivable shows that we have no way of verifying that it is in fact the real world – world number one – we are perceiving. Such doubts will always be possible so long as there remains a gap between the world we perceive and the world as it is. If we could verify the accuracy of our sensations by comparing them with the actual physical objects themselves, then such scepticism could be refuted instantly. But there can be no way of doing this. So even if, as above, we try to infer the existence of a material world by the fact that we are alive, such an inference can always be called into question; for we would still be making such an inference if there were no such world.

So the problem remains: if we perceive the world only indirectly, as representative realism claims, then we can never be absolutely sure of what the world is really like, or even if it is really out there at all.

■ **Figure 4.6 The veil of perception and the trap of solipsism**

All we have direct access to are our own sensations. We cannot peer beyond the veil of perception to perceive the world as it really is. But if we can't penetrate the veil of perception, then not only can we not know what the world is really like, but we can never know that the real world exists at all.

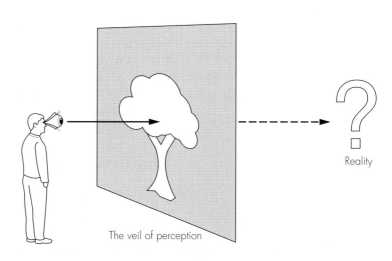

Reality

The veil of perception

Some philosophers have gone further still in analysing the consequences of this gap between sensation and reality.[47]

They claim that all the words and concepts we learn during our lives are learned by dealing with the world as we perceive it – the world of colours, smells, tastes and textures. As such, our concepts are designed to match and apply to this world of sensation. If this is the case, then there is no reason at all why our concepts should apply to world one – the world as it really is. For example, earlier we said that world one is the *cause* of our sensations. However, can we really say this? After all, the concept of causation is a concept that (as far as we can know) applies only to the world of sense experience. It is only within our experience that we observe one event causing another, but we can't observe the real world causing the perceived world, nor can we suppose the real world exhibits causal relations at all. The same applies to space and time. All of our sensations appear to us in space and time, but we cannot know whether the real world behind the veil is spatio-temporal. We, of course, can't imagine what a world would be like that did not involve space, time or causality. But that is to be expected, since we can only understand and imagine the world of our experience. The real world lies totally beyond our comprehension. We shouldn't even call it a world at all. We should say nothing about it whatsoever.[48]

Is there a physical world?

We have seen the representative realist introduce a gap between the nature of our experiences and the nature of the physical world in order to account for the possibility of sense-deception and the apparent fact that not everything we perceive is real. But in the process it has become unclear how to justify our claims to know things about a physical world that is supposed to exist independently of our experience. Sceptical doubts have forced us to retreat behind the veil of perception. If direct knowledge of the physical world is impossible and we can find no good reason to suppose that it exists at all, then belief in the external world begins to look like an irrational superstition, which any serious thinker must reject. This is the position of the solipsist. The solipsist has a rich interior life of her own sense experiences, but denies that anything exists other than such experiences. The universe of the solipsist is a purely mental universe of one.

Few, if any, philosophers have defended solipsism. This may be because any sincere solipsists would have no reason to write down their arguments since they would not believe there was anyone else around to read them. If I were ever to encounter someone defending solipsism I could be sure that they were mistaken since if I could understand their arguments then someone other than the solipsist (namely myself) must exist. But just because no one else could be correct in their solipsism doesn't refute it as a philosophical position. The possibility that no external world and no other minds exist remains a possibility for me, that is for the subject of experience. If solipsism is true, then what you are reading wasn't written by someone else – it is nothing more than an aspect of your consciousness.

How are you going to react to this possibility?

Anti-realist theories of perception

As we saw in our discussion of sceptical arguments earlier, there are two basic ways of reacting to the dilemmas they raise. One can either reject the sceptical conclusion and search for some flaw in the argument that leads to it, or one can accept the conclusion and attempt to explain away its apparent absurdity. An important line of response to the representative realist's problem takes this latter route. Anti-realists elect to swallow the sceptical conclusion, accepting that there is no reality existing independently of our experience. They hope to overcome the sceptical impasse by denying that there is any material world the existence of which we need to establish. The only reality is that of which we are *directly* aware, or what appears immediately to us; that is to say, sense data. Other than these apparent objects there is nothing left over, no EXTERNAL WORLD, for us to perceive indirectly. We will now look at two related anti-realist theories of perception – IDEALISM and PHENOMENALISM.

Idealism

Idealism is not simply a theory of perception. It is also an *ontology* – that is, a theory of being or of what exists. Ontology is the branch of philosophy concerned with working out what kinds of things there are, or of categorising the main ways or types of being. Although the idea of forming a theory of 'being' sounds daunting, it is plausible to hold that all of us have some implicit ontology, even if in most cases it is not well formalised. To try to work out what your ontology is, work through the following steps.

1 The first step is to think of everything that exists. Begin writing down everything you can think of. For example, you may begin like this:

My pen, my headache, myself, my neighbour's chickens, chicken pox, Chicken Tikka Massala, China, chamber music . . .

Now, obviously it is going to take too long to list literally *everything*, so to speed things along:

2 Try to lump similar types of thing together to produce different classes. Then make a list of the different classes you've created. For example, you may want to divide things into:

physical objects, people, concepts, sensations, animals, countries . . .

3 Once you've got what you think is an exhaustive list of the types of things there are, think about what each item on the list is ultimately made of, and write a list of the constituent ingredients. Keep reducing this list to the fewest basic ingredients. For example, you may find that ultimately:

all these things are made of physical matter, or thought.

When you have reduced this list to a few core ingredients and can reduce it no further then you are well on the way to formalising your own ontology. This ontology tells you what everything is ultimately made of.

As various philosophers over the ages have completed something akin to the above, three major ontologies have emerged:

Materialism   MATERIALISM is the view that everything in the world is made of matter. Dreams, countries, ideas, numbers, colours, and so on all boil down to matter in its various guises, interacting with other bits of matter.

Dualism   DUALISM claims that the list of things that exist can ultimately be reduced to two classes: *matter* – which occupies physical space, and *spirit or mind*, which is of a fundamentally different nature. This is, perhaps, the prevalent view on the planet, since many people believe that we, as humans, are made of a combination of a material body and a spiritual mind. Dualism's origins can be traced back before recorded history but it was Descartes in the modern era who gave it its most forceful philosophical expression.

Idealism   IDEALISM is the view that what is real depends upon the mind, and in the philosophy of perception it amounts to the claim that the material world does not exist outside of the mind. According to the idealist Berkeley, all that exists are minds and their ideas, sensations and thoughts. We know we have a mind, we know we perceive various colours and shapes, and so on. But to suppose that there is a material world that causes these sensations is a leap of faith that we do not need to make. To be an idealist is to take an anti-realist stance regarding matter.

■ Berkeley's idealism

Bishop George Berkeley was born in Ireland in 1685 and died in Oxford in 1753. During his life he made important contributions in the fields of philosophy, mathematics and economics. In philosophy he is considered the second of the three great British empiricists (the first being the Englishman John Locke and the third the Scot David Hume). He is most famous for founding the philosophy of idealism although his last writings were on the medicinal benefits of tar-water!

Berkeley termed sense data (and the other contents of the mind) IDEAS and claimed that physical objects don't exist independently of the mind, but in reality are collections of such ideas. This position he termed *idealism*.[49] Berkeley advanced several arguments for this position. The first follows from the empiricist principle he shared with Locke, namely that all the contents of our minds must come from experience.[50] Concepts, Berkeley is saying, have their origin in experience of sense data or 'ideas'. This means that if we think we have a concept, but can't find anything in experience whence it could have come, then we don't really have the concept at all. For example, a blind person, the empiricist argues, cannot have the concept of the colour red, since they have not had any experience of red.

With this point in view, let's consider the concept of matter. Where could this concept have come from? What is its basis in experience? Well, according to the representative realist, matter is something that we cannot experience since it lies beyond the veil of perception. It is the cause of our experience, but not something we can actually experience directly. But, Berkeley argues, if we accept that we cannot experience matter, then it follows from the empiricist principle that we cannot have a concept of it. In other words, the concept 'material object' is empty of content, for there is no possible experience, no possible sensation, from which we could have acquired it. For this reason he claimed that the representative realist's talk about 'matter' was literally meaningless and that the idea of an unperceivable thing was a contradiction in terms. From the claim that an object cannot exist unperceived, Berkeley concluded that its being or existence consists solely in its being perceived, or as he put it in Latin in his famous slogan: *esse est percipi*, meaning 'to be (or to exist) is to be perceived'.[51]

It is important to recognise that Berkeley did not intend to deny the existence of what we ordinarily think of as physical objects. Rather he is denying that they have an existence independent of sensation. He denies the existence of what the representative realist terms 'matter': some mysterious stuff which it is impossible to perceive. So an object, on Berkeley's account, is no more and no less than a cluster of ideas or sense data. An apple is a certain smell, taste, colour, shape, position and size, somehow bundled together before the mind.

Let's now return to the question of whether a tree makes a noise when falling in a forest if there is no one there to hear it, and ask how Berkeley answers it. Berkeley would claim that it makes no noise. Noises are ideas or sense data. They exist only in minds, and so if no mind is perceiving one, it does not exist. For similar reasons, there will be no colours, smells or tastes. However, Berkeley goes further and claims that there would be no actual tree falling at all unless someone experienced it. It's not just the noise which is perceived, but also the very event of the tree falling itself – the colours, the smells, the vibrations, and so on. The tree falling is no less something perceived than the noise we suppose it to make. We like to imagine that such a tree could still fall down unobserved, but when we do so we always do it from the point of view of an imaginary observer. To imagine the tree falling unobserved is implicitly to imagine its being observed. We are incapable of conceiving of the tree falling without at the same time conceiving the experience of the tree falling. For Berkeley this reinforces his point that to be is simply to be perceived.

An initial difficulty with idealism is that it seems unable to explain the distinction between perceptual error and *veridical*, i.e. truthful or accurate, perception. If everything we perceive is a kind of dream, as the idealist seems to be saying, then there would appear to be no difference between seeing something as it really is, and being mistaken; or between hallucinating and actually seeing something. But before we get too carried away with this apparent flaw, note that perceptual error is also a problem for the representative realist. The representative realist admits that we cannot distinguish hallucinations or errors from veridical (i.e. truthful) perception by appeal to the way the world really is in itself, since we have no access to such a world. This means that the distinction has to be made from within one's experience. Somehow or other we must make the distinction by examining the world of sense data or ideas, that is, by examining the contents of our own minds. In admitting this, the representative realist is obliged to give a similar solution to the idealist. However, at least the representative realist can make sense of the concept of perceptual error, as in their account there is a real physical world that our ideas represent, with fluctuating degrees of accuracy – hence error. The idealist does not have a 'real world' that can feature in their account of perceptual error. So the problem of accounting for error is a conceptual one.

Given this, how can the idealist make sense of perceptual error? The basic answer concerns the regularity that we observe in our past experience. We regard as real or veridical those features of what we perceive which fit well with the regularities displayed in our past experience, while those features which do not fit in well may be regarded as aberrations or errors. So, for example, if I perceive a pink elephant floating across my field of vision, I have a choice: I can regard it either as a veridical experience or as a hallucination. But I cannot determine this by comparing my sensations with the way the world is (as both idealist and representative realist admit). So I have to ask myself how well this experience fits in with my past experiences. Is this the kind of experience which coheres well with the way my world has been up to now? Clearly not, and so this is not to be regarded as a real feature of the world.

Criticisms of idealism

▶ criticism ◀ While the idealist seems to have explained the difference between illusions and veridical experiences, she still faces an obvious difficulty: what happens to objects when no one is perceiving them? The answer seems to be that they cease to exist. An apple, for example, no longer exists as soon as I hide it in a drawer, and yet, no sooner do I open the drawer once again than it miraculously returns to existence. Similarly, the apple has no smell or taste until someone smells and tastes it. Indeed, before someone bites into it it has no inside at all! But doesn't this seems patently absurd? You light a fire and it roars into life. You leave the room and thus it ceases to exist. You come back in the room and lo and behold, it exists again. Idealism seems to imply there are 'gaps' in the fire's existence when it is not perceived. But if fires are so 'gappy' how come the fire has dwindled as if it had existed all the time? What can the idealist say to explain this? Consider also the tree which falls unobserved in the forest. If we saw it standing one day, and on the ground the next, how did it get there? How do we explain this if there has been no process, no unobserved falling over that brought the tree to the ground? It seems that the world inhabited by the idealist is very different from the one to which we are used. Physical things have no hidden sides, no interiors, no secret aspects. They disappear and reappear without explanation, and there are no unobserved processes going on to explain the changes they undergo in the interim.

A related difficulty is that idealism appears not to be able to give any explanation of why there is such regularity and predictability in our experience, nor where our ideas come from. Why, for example, do I expect to see the apple once again on reopening the drawer? Why can I be pretty sure of how this apple will taste? Indeed why do I see and hear things at all? The realist of whatever stripe claims to have a good explanation of why we have the sense data we do and why they are so regular and predictable. There exist material objects which impact upon our sense organs and cause us to see, hear or taste them. Matter retains certain properties when we are not perceiving it, so when we do come to perceive it we can expect it to produce the same sensations in us. It is because of the independent existence of matter that our experience hangs together as it does. Idealism appears to have no parallel explanation, and the whole world of ideas we inhabit appears nothing short of miraculous.

■ Berkeley's defence

In response to the complaint that idealism cannot explain the regularity of our experience, Berkeley would simply question the materialist's use of matter to this end. Why, he would ask, should we suppose matter to behave in a regular way? What account does the materialist have of this? Isn't this at least as miraculous as Berkeley's claim that our sensations exhibit regularity? So when it comes to explaining regularity, materialism and idealism are in the same boat.

But what of the gappiness of objects? Berkeley's idealism as so far characterised appears to fly in face of our common-sense understanding of the nature of physical things, and threatens to reduce idealism to absurdity. Berkeley takes the challenge seriously and salvages his account by supposing that there is an all-powerful God who is a permanent perceiver of all possible ideas. By perceiving everything when no humans or animals are perceiving them, Berkeley's God ensures that physical objects retain the kind of continuous existence that realists and common sense would claim for them. This also explains both the origin and regularity of our sense data. Berkeley's defence is neatly summed up in a limerick by Ronald Knox:[52]

> *There was a young man who said, 'God*
> *Must think it exceedingly odd*
> *If he finds that this tree*
> *Continues to be*
> *When there is no one around in the Quad.'*

To which the reply is:

> *Dear Sir:*
> *Your astonishment's odd:*
> *I am always around in the Quad,*
> *And that's why the tree*
> *Will continue to be*
> *Since observed by*
> > *Yours faithfully*
> > > *God*

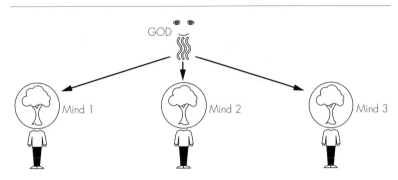

Nothing can exist unperceived. So physical objects are just collections of 'ideas' or sense data appearing to minds. God plants these ideas in all of us and perceives the world, thereby keeping it in existence.

Criticisms of Berkeley

▶ criticism ◀

The use of God to shore up a philosophical position is often regarded as evidence that there is something seriously wrong with it. God helps Berkeley out of his difficulties but we have no independent reason to suppose either that there is a God or, if there is, that he plays the role Berkeley casts him in. To use God in this way to expressly solve a problem is often regarded as intellectually dishonest since it masquerades as an explanation while in fact explains nothing. If whenever there is something that we can't explain we turn to divine intervention, then we could eliminate all mysteries. All philosophical difficulties could be explained away as miracles; a bit like 'solving' a puzzle about the world by explaining sagely that God moves in mysterious ways.

Before leaving Berkeley let's allow him the last word in defence of his theory. While the materialist thinks his use of God is dishonest, at least God is supposed to be an intelligence, and so it makes sense that he would do things in an orderly way. So he provides a good explanation of the regularity and predictability of experience. The idea that some mindless substance called matter should behave in a regular and orderly fashion and so account for the origin and regularity of experience is, according to Berkeley, a far bigger cop out than appeal to God. In fact, it's worth noting that as far as Berkeley is concerned, God doesn't enter his theory to save it. Rather Berkeley's whole argument amounts to a demonstration of God's existence. If his arguments succeed in showing that matter cannot exist, then the only way to explain the orderly appearance of sense data is by positing the existence of some intelligence producing them.

Below are four well-known objections to Berkeley's idealism.

1 Read through each quotation in turn and see if you can work out what objection is being made.

2 Ask yourself how Berkeley might respond.

3 Finally decide who you think is right.

---

a) From James Boswell's *Life of Johnson*

After we came out of the church, we stood talking for some time together of Bishop Berkeley's ingenious sophistry to prove the non-existence of matter, and that every thing in the universe is merely ideal. I observed that though we are satisfied his doctrine is not true, it is impossible to refute it. I never shall forget the alacrity with which Johnson answered, striking his foot with mighty force against a large stone, till he rebounded from it, 'I refute it thus.'[53]

---

b) From James Boswell's *Life of Johnson*

Being in company with a gentleman who thought fit to maintain Dr Berkeley's ingenious philosophy, that nothing exists but as perceived by some mind; when the gentleman was going away, Johnson said to him, 'Pray, Sir, don't leave us; for we may perhaps forget to think of you, and then you will cease to exist.'[54]

---

c) From G. E. Moore's 'Proof of an External World'

I can now give a large number of different proofs [of the existence of things outside of us], each of which is a perfectly rigorous proof [. . .] I can prove now, for instance, that two human hands exist. How? By holding up my two hands, and saying, as I make a certain gesture with the right hand, 'Here is one hand', and adding, as I make a certain gesture with the left, 'and here is another'. And if, by doing this, I have proved *ipso facto* the existence of external things, you will all see that I can also do it now in numbers of other ways: there is no need to multiply examples.[55]

---

d) From David Hume's *A Treatise on Human Nature*

Thus the sceptic still continues to reason and believe, even tho' he asserts that he cannot defend his reason by reason; and by the same rule he must assent to the principle concerning the existence of body, tho' he cannot pretend by any argument of philosophy to maintain its veracity. Nature has not left this to his choice, and has doubtless esteem'd it of far too great importance to be trusted to our uncertain reasonings and speculations. We may well ask, What causes induce us to believe in the existence of body? But 'tis in vain to ask, Whether there be body or not? That is a point, which we must take for granted in all our reasonings.[56]

Phenomenalism

Despite the evident difficulties facing an anti-realist theory of perception, attempts at crafting a plausible theory did not die with Berkeley. Phenomenalism is a nineteenth- and twentieth-century attempt at updating Berkeley's insights. Phenomenalists attempted to improve on idealism by offering a more plausible explanation of both the occurrence of sense data, and their regularity. According to this view, objects are collections not just of *actual* sense data – or what phenomenalists now call 'phenomena' meaning appearances – but also of *possible* ones. Its claim is that physical objects exist unperceived so long as they retain the potential to be perceived. So the reason my apple reappears when I reopen the drawer is that it remained possible to see it for anyone who cared to look. Or as J. S. Mill put it: 'Matter [. . .] may be defined, a Permanent Possibility of Sensation.'[57] In fact, the seeds of this idea are already there in Berkeley when he suggests that we can say that physical objects exist so long as it is *possible* to see them, even though they may not actually be perceived.[58]

In sum, where the idealist says that to be (i.e. to exist) is to be perceived, the phenomenalist says that to be is to be *perceivable*. So long as objects are capable of being perceived, even if they are not actually being perceived at the moment, they exist. Returning to our tree in the forest, the phenomenalist says that it both falls and makes a sound although no one is there to see or hear it, just because if someone had been there they would have seen and heard it.

One variation of phenomenalism that gained particular favour is *linguistic phenomenalism*. Linguistic phenomenalism is primarily a theory of meaning: it's a theory about what we really mean when we talk about physical objects. The linguistic phenomenalist claims that although we talk quite happily about physical objects as if they exist, when we do so we are in fact referring to various patterns of sense data that we experience. Talk of physical objects is just a shorthand way of talking about collections of sense data or phenomena. As such, linguistic phenomenalism claims that, although useful, talk of physical objects can technically be avoided as it is only really sense data to which we are referring. So linguistic phenomenalism amounts to the claim that all talk of independently existing objects can be translated into talk about sense data without any loss of meaning. Such a claim is backed up by considering how we learn language. We are born and slowly start to perceive lots of strange shapes, colours, noises and tastes. As young babies we start to recognise familiar patterns in these colours and shapes and eventually we learn to associate a word with these patterns, such as 'apple', 'dog' or 'shoe horn'. Slowly our vocabulary increases, but ultimately all the words we learn for the objects around us are really just words for regular and consistent patterns of sense data. Talk about physical objects is thus just a shorthand for talk about sense data. So the word 'apple' doesn't really refer to some independent material object, it really means something like 'round, red and green, hard, sweet, slightly sharp, crunchy, etc. etc. collection of potential sense data'.

To illustrate this, consider a character such as Buzz Lightyear from the computer-animated film *Toy Story*. We have no difficulty in talking about him or about other characters in the film, and yet we are simply referring to a particular collection of coloured shapes on the screen and the sounds that accompany them. 'Buzz Lightyear' is just the name for this collection of colours and sounds, and he has no existence independently of it. The phenomenalist is saying that the same principle applies to everything you perceive. All objects are just collections of sense data. They have no independent existence.

If the translation of talk about physical objects into talk about sense data is to work, there must be no loss of meaning between the original and the translation. Just as a translation of a French expression into English shouldn't retain any French words, so there must be no physical object expressions left over in the translation from physical object language into 'phenomenal' or 'sense data language'.

Here is an example of how a phenomenal translation might work. The physical object expression:

- *The melon rolls across the wooden table and knocks over a glass.*

becomes:

- *A round yellow patch rotates and moves left across the brown expanse reaching a transparent, hard container-shaped collection of sense data which turns suddenly downwards.*

The first phrase features the word 'melon', 'table' and 'glass'. These could be construed as referring to independently existing objects, whereas in the translation we are clearly referring only to patterns of sense data, and at no point is the existence of independent objects implied. Note that phenomenalists are not saying that we should all start talking in *phenomenalese*. Obviously this would be impractical since it would take too long and communication would break down. Rather they are arguing that it is possible to remove all talk of physical objects from our speech with no loss of meaning. It may be long-winded and unwieldy, but ultimately it means exactly the same. If this is right it shows that belief in the existence of independent physical objects is redundant. In principle at least we can make do with sense data alone.

experimenting with ideas

1 To get the hang of this idea, try your hand at your own translations of the following terms into *phenomenalese*:
   a) boiled egg
   b) tomato
   c) banana.
2 What difficulties did you encounter?
3 While long-winded, you probably found that translating a single word is relatively easy. But now consider translating full sentences.

   The boiled egg fell into the bowl of water with a splash.

   How did you do?

The linguistic phenomenalist can also deal with the problem faced by idealism of explaining what we mean when we talk about objects that are not currently being perceived. We really mean that they would be perceived if there were someone suitably placed to perceive them. For example, the sentence:

■ *There is an unobserved tree falling in the forest.*

really means something like:

■ *If you approached the large green and brown expanse (the forest) and walked into it for a while, then a small brown and green patch (the tree) would shift in relation to the other brown and green patches and a roaring noise and shaking would also be experienced.*

The phenomenalist is saying that, instead of explaining perception by reference to the independent existence of material objects as the realist does, we should appeal to continuing possibilities of experience; possibilities which will be triggered by the occurrence of suitable conditions. If someone happens to be in the right place at the right time they will have experiences of a certain sort. This remains true whether or not anyone is in such a time and place. This means that the phenomenalist explains my seeing a tree by appealing to the statement that '*if* suitable conditions were to obtain (the tree is before me, the lighting conditions are good, I have normal vision, etc.), *then* I would have tree-seeing-experiences, *and* those conditions do obtain'. It is the truth of this statement that explains why I have the sense experiences I do. Similarly, she explains my *not* seeing the tree, although it continues to exist hidden in the forest, by claiming that this simply means that *if* suitable conditions were to obtain (if I were to go to the forest, stand before the tree, in good lighting conditions, with good eyesight, etc.), *then* I would see the tree, but presently these conditions do not obtain.

'*If . . . then*' STATEMENTS of this sort are called HYPOTHETICAL since they make claims about states of affairs which are not actual, but which would be if certain conditions were satisfied. When we talk of the independent existence of objects which are not being perceived, all that we really mean is that certain hypothetical statements are true. So we don't mean to be making claims about entities existing unperceived, rather we are talking about what we would perceive under certain conditions. Clearly, hypothetical statements are going to be central to any complete phenomenal translation since we can never perceive every possible aspect of an object at any time. By using such hypothetical statements we can translate all our talk about material objects into talk about actual and potential sense data. Such a translation is often termed a *reduction*.

experimenting with ideas

With this in view, try some further phenomenal translations using hypothetical sentences.

a) The soft boiled egg is in the pan.
b) You are never more than a metre from a rat.
c) There is a maggot in the apple.

One benefit of phenomenalism is that its anti-realist position makes it resistant to sceptical attack since it closes the gap between our experience and the world. For the realist there is always the lurking sceptical question, 'How can I be sure there really is a table in this room?' or 'Perhaps I am being deceived or having a dream?' Phenomenalism can dismiss such worries. In saying 'there is a table in the room' the phenomenalist simply means: 'If I were to look in the room, then I would have table-like experiences' and this is true whether dreaming or not. The sceptic can only make hay if there is a possible gap between conscious experience and the world on which to cast doubt. But the phenomenalist is saying that all talk about the world is really talk about experience, so there is no gap for the sceptic to exploit.

Criticisms of phenomenalism

▶ criticism ◀ Despite its advantages, we may still harbour the same worries over this form of anti-realism as we did over idealism. Simply to say that an object is a 'permanent possibility of sensation' isn't much of an explanation either of the occurrence of perceptual experience or of its regularity. Surely the realists' explanation still has the advantage, since they claim that as well as the permanent possibility of experience there is a permanent ground for that possibility, something distinct from and supporting it – namely the material world. Another way of posing this worry is to ask what makes the phenomenalists' hypothetical statements true. Where the realist can readily answer this by appealing to a continuous material object, the phenomenalist appears able only to throw up her hands. Isn't this the same miracle that Berkeley needed to bring in God to explain?

The standard phenomenalist reply is to appeal to regularities in past experience. The hypothetical statement that someone would see the tree if they looked in the forest is justified by the regular ways in which trees have been experienced in the past. In other words, if every time in the past that you've gone for a walk in the forest you've had the same pattern of tree-like experiences, then this justifies you in making the general hypothetical claim that if you were to go once more to the forest you would once again have the same tree-like experiences. A statement of regularity, in other words, is good evidence for the truth of a hypothetical.

▶ criticism ◀ However, such a response may still strike us as an inadequate account of the actual nature of our perceptual experience. If we ask why a particular situation should produce certain experiences, an appeal to past regularities is not what we are after. Rather, we are asking for the cause. The reason why the tree reappears every time I go on the same walk in the forest cannot be that it has appeared in the past under similar circumstances. This may be the evidence we would appeal to in order to justify our expectation that it will reappear, but it is not an explanation of why it will: it is not the underlying cause. Past regularities, in other words, don't constitute an object's existence unperceived. Instead, says the realist, the independent existence of the object explains the regularities. So the tree doesn't reappear because it has reappeared in the past, rather it has reappeared in the past because it was there all along. For the realist, the phenomenalist just gets things the wrong way around.

Once again, the phenomenalist has a reply. She may seek to question whether the realists' appeal to material objects is really any better as an explanation of regularity. Can't we ask the same questions of matter as the realist asks of phenomena? Why should matter retain the properties it does so as to be ready on occasion to provide us with predictable sense data? Isn't the appeal to matter with its regular properties just as miraculous as an appeal to regularities in possible sense data? The only possible justification for supposing that matter will retain its properties unperceived is because of past regularities, and so the realist is in the same boat as the phenomenalist when it comes to explaining why experience is as it is.

▶ criticism ◀ Another line of criticism of phenomenalism concerns the impossibility of translating all talk about objects into talk about sense data. Consider the physical object statement:

■ *There is a machine gun beneath the window in the room next door.*

For the phenomenalist all this talk of objects is really just talk of sense data, so the statement would translate into something like this:

■ *If you left this room, turned right and walked down the corridor and into the next room then you would have window-like experiences; and then, if you approached the window-like experiences and looked down, then you would have machine gun-like experiences.*

However, in doing all this, the second statement is describing a situation that still involves physical objects such as rooms and corridors. So clearly the translation is not yet complete, and all such talk must be further reduced to talk about sense data. The hypothetical statement must be expanded to include descriptions of 'walking-down-corridor-like experiences' and 'room-like experiences'. But having done all this our hypothetical statement still involves spatial relations, such as turning right, being next to or looking down. How are we going to translate these in terms of actual or potential sense data? The difficulty is that each hypothetical statement that we use is talking about what an observer would perceive under certain conditions. But these conditions have to be characterised in terms of physical objects and spatial relations. The observer has to be in some appropriate position in order to perceive, and this means being spatially related to the object in question and using one's physical sense organs. Whatever we try, it seems we are going to end up reintroducing spatial relations and our own bodies into the translation. So any phenomenal translation will be not only infinitely complex and long but also impossible, even in principle, to complete since it must reintroduce physical object language at each turn. This seems to show that our language is dependent on the assumption of an independently existing world and cannot be translated into statements about actual and potential sense data.

▶ criticism ◀ Another difficulty concerns the supposed incorrigibility of the sense data, which are supposed to form the basis for our understanding of the world. This thesis, to recap, states that while we can be mistaken about our perception of material objects, the same is not the case for sense data. Sense data are appearances, and appearances cannot appear differently from the way they are. This is why Descartes felt that one could be absolutely certain of the content of one's own mind, but any judgement about objects lying beyond the mind could be open to doubt. The problem arises, however, when we consider that sense data can appear *indeterminate*. Often I may not have any determinate idea of the colour of someone's eyes while I am talking to them. In such a case it would seem peculiar to say that their eyes had no determinate colour at all, for surely all visible sensations must have some colour. Similarly with my perception, for example, of a figure with several sides. If the number of sides is high enough I will probably be unable to determine exactly how many it is. But if the figure is as it appears then it would seem to follow that the figure must actually have an indeterminate number of sides. This seems to be absurd since a number cannot be indeterminate in itself. So this suggests that we cannot even characterise the way things appear to us in any clear way, and so cannot expect the language of sense data to be the original into which all other talk should be reduced.

experimenting with ideas

On the next page are summarised the main theses of the three principal theories of perception we have been studying.

1 Read through each thesis and be sure you understand what it is saying.
2 Try to formulate an argument against each of the theses in turn.
3 Write down the argument. Be clear about the distinction between the *conclusion* of your argument and the *evidence* you are using to support it.

a) *Naïve realism*
   i) Physical objects exist in space and have the properties we perceive them to have.
   ii) We perceive physical objects directly because they are there and we know they are there because we perceive them directly.
   iii) When no one is perceiving an object it continues to exist along with all its properties.

b) *Representative realism*
   i) Physical objects exist in space and have only some of the properties we perceive them to have.
   ii) We perceive our own sense data directly, and physical objects only indirectly.
   iii) When no one is perceiving an object it continues to exist along with some of its properties.

c) *Berkeley's idealism*
   i) Physical objects are clusters of sense data or ideas existing in minds.
   ii) An object exists only when someone is perceiving it (idealism).
   iii) God perceives everything and so sustains the universe in existence.

d) *Phenomenalism*
   i) Physical objects are permanent possibilities of sensation.
   ii) All talk about physical objects can be reduced to talk about sense data without loss of meaning.
   iii) We are able to predict what sense data we will perceive because of past regularities in experience.

Conclusion

One might have thought that there could be nothing easier in life than simply sensing and experiencing the world. Opening our eyes to see or our ears to hear normally requires no real effort. However, we have seen that trying to account for the relationship between our sense experiences and the world is far from easy. The natural view – the view of common sense or naïve realism – that we peer out through our eyes and listen through our ears and simply see and hear the world around us as it is, turned out not to hold water. Having done what Hume calls 'the slightest philosophy', we saw that the world cannot be exactly as it appears and that perception is a complex affair. Our eyes receive light reflected off objects and this triggers a complex chain of events involving the optic nerve and the visual cortex (at the back of the head), which culminates in the experience of seeing an object. In the process our senses interpret the world for us and present us with a picture of it, which may be accurate in some respects but deceptive in others. This recognition appeared to lead us to the view that these experiences or sense data exist only in our minds, that they are representations of the world which enable us to interact with it. This is the view of representative realism.

But such a view drives a wedge between our sensations and reality (see Figure 4.6). Now there seem to be two worlds involved: the world as we perceive it, full of colours and sounds, and the world as it really is in itself, a bumbling mass of colourless, soundless matter or energy. It appears that we can no longer be certain that our senses give us genuine knowledge of the world, as we can never check our sensations against reality. Any attempt to do so can only give us further sensations. A 'veil of perception' has descended between us and the world which it seems impossible to remove.

This difficulty led some thinkers to suggest that the very belief that there is an independent world causing our sensations is the problem. Idealists hoped to do away with belief in matter, regarding it is as leap of faith that we do not need to make. However, idealism itself seems to rely on a leap of religious faith. As we saw, Berkeley is forced to rely on God to explain why it is that we have the regular experiences that we do, and why we suppose objects to exist when no one perceives them. Phenomenalism seemed to fare better, but still the worry remained that we need some explanation of the regularity and predictability of experience. Moreover, as we argued, the project to translate all talk about physical objects into sense data needs to reintroduce a commitment to a physical world. Matter, it seems, is not so easily dismissed.

It seems that any account of perception runs into profound difficulty. The simple act of perceiving the world turns out to be one of the hardest for which to give an accurate account.

Key points: Chapter 4

What you need to know about **knowledge and perception**:

1 Naïve realism is the common-sense view of perception. It is a realist theory because it claims that physical objects exist independently of our perception of them. The properties of objects, from their size and shape through to colours, smells and textures, also have independent existence and are perceived directly by us.

2 However, naïve realism finds it difficult to account for sense deception, and the apparent fact that physical objects often appear different from how they really are. Also, some of the properties perceived in objects seem not to be really out there, but are effects on perceiving beings like ourselves.

3 Various considerations lead philosophers to draw a distinction between properties that actually exist in objects themselves, and the powers these objects have to produce sensations of various sorts in us. Those such as size, position and shape are real and are known as primary qualities. Those such as colour, sound and smell are called secondary qualities.

4 Representative realism claims that physical objects impact upon our sense organs, causing us to experience sensations. These sensations are akin to pictures which represent the objects that cause them. So we don't perceive the world directly, but indirectly, via our sensations.

5 This view, however, also leads into difficulties. If we are directly acquainted only with our own sensations, and have only indirect access to the real world, the question arises of how we can be certain that we are perceiving the world accurately. Moreover, as we are caught behind the veil of perception, the trap of solipsism looms.

6 Berkeley tried to deal with the problems of representative realism by denying that there is any material world about which doubt might arise. True to his empiricist principles, he argued that the concept of something which could not be experienced is incoherent, and so the idea of a material world lying beyond the veil of perception had to be dismissed. To exist, something had to be perceived, and so physical things can exist only when perceived by some mind.

7 Berkeley's anti-realism faces an immediate difficulty, namely how to account for our ordinary sense that physical objects continue to exist when no one is perceiving them. Berkeley's answer is that God perceives everything and so sustains the universe in existence.

8 Berkeley's use of God, however, looks like a desperate measure to save his theory. Phenomenalism offers an alternative way of explaining the persistence of objects unperceived: they continue to exist so long as they remain perceivable. Physical objects are thus reduced to actual and potential sense data.

9 For the linguistic phenomenalist this means that all statements about physical objects can be translated into hypothetical statements about what would be perceived if one were to be in the appropriate situation.

10 Phenomenalism also faces its difficulties however. One significant problem is that it would seem that our efforts to translate physical object language into phenomenal language will always reintroduce physical objects.

5 The concept of knowledge

Introduction

Philosophers have often felt that before they could produce a proper theory of knowledge they would need to get clear what they were theorising about. Without a good idea of what something is, one cannot say much of interest about it. Accordingly, epistemology often begins with the question of what precisely knowledge is. However, going against this trend, we have left the analysis of what 'knowledge' actually means until last. By first exploring the problems of epistemology, we hope to have sharpened our understanding of what knowledge is in advance of attempting to home in on a definition. The term 'knowledge', however, doesn't have just one meaning, and philosophers have traditionally divided knowledge into three main types.

1 Practical knowledge

This is knowledge of how to do something. For example, we talk of knowing how to swim, of how to speak Russian, or of how to bake a soufflé. Such knowledge involves a capacity to perform a certain kind of task, but need not involve having any explicit understanding of what such a performance entails. In other words, I may know how to swim without being able to explain how. I may know how to tie my shoelaces, while giving verbal instructions would be extremely hard. So it is possible to know how to do things, without being able to articulate our knowledge, suggesting that practical knowledge is independent of any ability to communicate it in language or of having any conscious knowledge of precisely what one knows.

2 Knowledge by acquaintance

This is knowing in the sense of knowing a person, place or thing. So, for example, we often speak of knowing somebody because we have met them, or knowing Paris in virtue of having visited it, or knowing the taste of pineapple having tried it. As with practical knowledge, knowledge by acquaintance need not involve any capacity to give a verbal report of what it entails. I may know the taste of pineapple without being able to describe it and without knowing any facts about it. (We saw earlier that empiricists regard knowledge by acquaintance with our own sense data as the foundation of all empirical knowledge.)

3 Factual knowledge

This is knowing that something is the case. So, for example, we speak of knowing that squirrels collect nuts in autumn, that the Earth orbits the sun, or that Socrates was a philosopher. Unlike the other two types of knowledge, when we know some fact, what we know can, in principle, be expressed in language. Thus if someone claims to know that Socrates was a philosopher, he or she claims that the sentence 'Socrates was a philosopher' is true. What is asserted by a sentence, that is to say, what it means or affirms about the world, is called a *proposition* and for this reason factual knowledge is often called *propositional* knowledge.[59] It's interesting to note that knowledge by acquaintance and factual knowledge are distinguished in many languages. French, for example, has *connaître* and *savoir*, German has both *kennen* and *wissen*, whereas English just has *to know*.

Because factual knowledge is expressed in language it involves holding *beliefs*, unlike practical knowledge or knowledge by acquaintance. If I have knowledge of certain facts, I *believe* certain propositions to be true; in other words, I *assent* to these propositions. Because it deals with knowing facts, and so with having beliefs that can be either true or false, it is the kind of knowledge with which philosophers have been primarily concerned. Before proceeding to analyse factual knowledge it will be necessary to clarify what is meant by some of the key terms, namely 'belief', 'proposition', 'fact' and 'truth'. These are terms which in ordinary English have somewhat ambiguous meanings, and so if we are to make headway in our analysis of knowledge it is important that we give working definitions of these terms (see Figure 5.1 opposite).

The chapter is divided as follows:

- Factual knowledge
- Knowledge as justified, true belief (JTB)
- Are the JTB conditions individually necessary?
- Are the JTB conditions jointly sufficient?
- Gettier-type objections to the traditional analysis
- Conclusion
- Key points you need to know about the concept of knowledge.

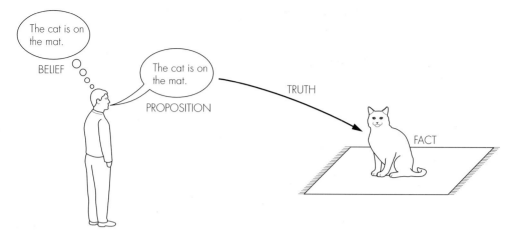

Figure 5.1 Beliefs, propositions and facts

- A *belief* is a thought which is about the world. It is a mental representation which claims that something is the case. Beliefs can be true or false. In the figure, Sam has the belief that the cat is on the mat.

- A *proposition* is what a statement says or asserts about the world. Like beliefs, propositions can be true or false. When Sam utters the sentence 'The cat is on the mat' he is expressing the proposition that the cat is on the mat.

- A FACT is something that is the case in the world. Here the fact is the cat's being on the mat. Facts can't be true or false, they just are.

- TRUTH is a tricky concept, but one account of truth is that it involves a correspondence between a belief or a proposition and the world. If Sam's belief that the cat is on the mat corresponds with the world, i.e. with the facts, then it is true. So his belief will be true if the cat is indeed on the mat.

Factual knowledge

What, then, is factual knowledge? A question like this is hard to answer directly. It is difficult even to know how to begin. A promising approach, first adopted by Plato, is to ask what must be the case when someone knows something. Under what circumstances do we say that someone has knowledge? To answer this question we will look for the conditions or criteria which would establish that someone knows a proposition. If we can list these conditions and so say exactly when someone does and doesn't know something, then we will have a pretty good idea of what knowledge is.

In order to clarify this approach it will be useful to abbreviate the expression 'someone knows a proposition' to 'S knows that p'. Here 'S' stands for the subject (the person doing the knowing – for example, Sharon), and 'p' for the proposition that she knows (for example, that Paris is the capital of France). So we need to determine what conditions must be satisfied in order for us to assert 'S knows that p' (Sharon knows that Paris is the capital of France).

ACTIVITY **1** To get started on our search for a definition of 'knowledge' let's try to distinguish it from belief. Begin by writing a short list of things you would normally claim to *know*, and another of things you merely *believe*. These may be things that you know or believe have happened or exist. Try not to be too influenced by the sceptical arguments we've looked at before and simply use the terms 'know' and 'believe' as they would be used in everyday life.

2 Having done this, consider what has to be the case for you to claim that you know something as opposed to simply believing it. What makes the knowledge claims different from the belief claims? Now read on to see how your answer compares with Plato's.

Plato on true belief and knowledge

Having begun to think about the differences between knowledge and belief, we can now examine how Plato approached the problem. In his dialogue, the *Meno*, he tries to work out the difference between someone having a true belief and someone having knowledge. He begins by pointing out that true belief has much in common with knowledge. Indeed, it would seem that the two are equally valuable as guides to action. Socrates, the character expounding Plato's views, explains his reasoning to his interlocutor Meno as follows:

Socrates:	*Let me explain. If someone knows the way to Larissa, or anywhere else you like, then when he goes there and takes others with him he will be a good and capable guide, you would agree?*
Meno:	*Of course.*
Socrates:	*But if a man judges correctly which is the road, though he has never been there and doesn't know it, will he not also guide others aright?*
Meno:	*Yes, he will.*
Socrates:	*And as long as he has a correct belief on the points about which the other has knowledge, he will be just as good a guide, believing the truth but not knowing it.*
Meno:	*Just as good.*
Socrates:	*Therefore true belief is as good a guide as knowledge for the purpose of acting rightly.*[60]

Here Plato is arguing that so long as my beliefs are true then they are as useful to me and to others as if I had knowledge. So why, the question arises, should we prefer knowledge to true belief? Are they in fact the same thing and if so why is knowledge so highly prized? Socrates' answer has many facets, but we will focus on the next page on one aspect, which contrasts the stability of knowledge with the flightiness of belief.

Socrates:	*True beliefs are a fine thing and do all sorts of good so long as they stay in their place; but they will not stay long. They run away from a man's mind, so they are not worth much until you tether them by working out the reason. [. . .] Once they are tied down, they become knowledge, and are stable. That is why knowledge is something more valuable than right belief. What distinguishes one from the other is the tether.[61]*

This all sounds rather cryptic, as Plato readily accepts.[62] What can he mean by beliefs failing to 'stay in their place'? What is to 'tether them by working out the reason'? Plato seems to be saying that part of the reason we value knowledge is that it is more steadfast than mere belief since it is backed up by reasons or evidence. The evidence acts as a kind of glue, which retains the belief in the mind by giving us good reason to continue believing it. By contrast, a belief for which we have no evidence – even if it happens to be true – has nothing to make it stick in the mind. If I have no good reason for believing a proposition, it will not take much for someone to dissuade me from it. But if I know it, I will not readily withdraw my assent.

So Plato is suggesting that it is a kind of tethering that converts belief into knowledge. To have knowledge is to have a true belief secured by reasons. In another dialogue, the *Theaetetus*, Plato offers other considerations in support of the idea that knowledge is more than mere true belief.

Socrates:	*Now, when a jury has been persuaded, fairly, of things which no one but an eyewitness could possibly know, then, in reaching a decision based on hearsay, they do so without knowledge, but get hold of true belief, given that their verdict is fair because what they have been made to believe is correct.*
Theaetetus:	*Absolutely.*
Socrates:	*But if true belief and knowledge were identical, my friend, then even the best juryman in the world would never form a correct belief, but fail to have knowledge; so it looks as though they are different.[63]*

Plato's point here is that we can hold true beliefs that we would be reluctant to call knowledge because of the nature of the evidence supporting them. A juror can come to a correct decision on the balance of evidence presented in court. But if the evidence available to him were circumstantial and less than absolutely conclusive we would be reluctant to call this knowledge. By contrast, an eyewitness to the events in question could indeed be said to know. Consider also the example of a gambler who believes that the next number on the roulette wheel will be red. Even if he happens to be right, we would be reluctant to say that he truly knew.

These examples show that the manner by which one acquires a true belief, or by which one *justifies* it, is important to its counting as a piece of knowledge. Because of basic considerations such as this, Plato is led in the *Theaetetus* to consider the view that 'true belief accompanied by a rational account is knowledge',[64] or as we might say, knowledge is a *justified, true belief* – that is, a true belief for which the believer has adequate reasons or evidence.

So it seems we have an early candidate for a definition of factual knowledge. Someone knows something if they have a belief that is true, and that has a good justification.

1 Think up your own examples, like those above, to illustrate the difference between having a true belief and having knowledge.

2 The last activity (on page 126) involved writing down some things you claimed to believe and other things that you claimed to know. Go back to these statements and see if the missing ingredient in the two cases is indeed the degree of justification for the belief.

Knowledge as justified, true belief

The definition of knowledge as justified, true belief is the traditional one. If it is correct, it means that if someone knows a proposition, then three conditions must be satisfied. The person must *believe* the proposition, it must be *true*, and it must be *justified*. These conditions can be set out as follows:

> S knows that p if and only if: (e.g. *Sharon knows that Paris is the capital of France if and only if . . .*)
> 1 S believes that p (*the belief condition; e.g. Sharon believes Paris is the capital of France*)
> 2 p is true (*the truth condition; e.g. Paris is indeed the capital of France*)
> 3 S has adequate or sufficient evidence for p, or is justified in believing p (*the evidence condition; e.g. Sharon read that Paris is the capital of France in an encyclopedia*).

This means that the proposition 'S knows that p' is true if and only if S believes that p, p is true and S has adequate justification for her belief. These three conditions are said to be individually NECESSARY AND jointly SUFFICIENT for saying that 'S knows that p'. So you need each one to have knowledge and if you have all three then you definitely have knowledge. This kind of definition of a concept is what philosophers call a *logical analysis* of the concept.

1 Read the scenarios given below. Using your common-sense intuitions decide in each case whether the person in bold knows the fact in question.

2 Check to see whether:

   a) the person believes the fact (the belief condition)

   b) the fact is true (the truth condition)

   c) the person would be justified in believing it (the evidence condition).

---

a) **Davina** thinks that monkeys are more intelligent than humans because her mate told her so.

b) **Ravi** reckons the sun will set at 19:02 on Sunday having read as much in the paper. And it does.

c) The forecast says there is a 50–50 chance of rain tomorrow. Looking at the sky, **farmer Pete** is convinced it will be dry. It stays dry the whole day.

d) Having been told by his parents and having read books and watched videos on the subject, young **Victor** is convinced that Santa Claus exists.

e) **Hamid** is convinced that Pluto is the furthest planet from the sun because Mickey Mouse told him so in a dream.

f) **Tamsin** learns from a textbook that *Hamlet* is Shakespeare's longest play (which it is).

g) **Wanda** watches five videos of Shakespeare plays and concludes by their length that *Hamlet* must be Shakespeare's longest play.

h) Colin is going out with Simone. However at a party he drunkenly, yet inexcusably, gets off with Fiona. No one sees a thing. Back at college Nigel is secretly in love with Simone. To try to get Simone and Colin to split up he makes up a rumour, telling Brian that Colin and Fiona got off at the party. Later on **Chanise** hears this rumour and believes it.

---

3 If all three conditions are met then according to the JTB analysis this should be a case of knowledge. If one or more of the conditions are not met, then this is not a case of knowledge. Did using the three conditions match your own intuitions in each of the cases?

4 Consider whether justified, true belief is a good analysis of the concept of knowledge. What problems could the definition run into? How good must the justification be? (Remember: we are looking to establish the criteria for the everyday concept of knowledge, and justification need not be perfect for knowledge to be claimed in everyday parlance. So avoid ruling out examples just because absolute certainty is not established.)

In the activity you have been testing the justified, true belief (JTB) analysis of knowledge. In other words, you have been considering whether each condition is necessary by asking whether we can do without belief, truth or justification. You may also have considered a slightly different question when you got to scenario h), namely whether or not together the conditions are sufficient. In other words, you may have been wondering whether someone who has all three conditions definitely has knowledge. It's important to recognise that these two questions are distinct.

In the following discussion of the traditional analysis of knowledge we will treat each question separately. First, we will ask whether the three conditions are *individually necessary*. This means seeing whether we need each one by seeing if we can do without any. Second, we will examine whether they are *jointly sufficient*. This means seeing whether having all three definitely guarantees you have knowledge, and involves looking at odd cases where someone seems to have a justified, true belief, but not knowledge.

Are the JTB conditions individually necessary?

1 The belief condition

The belief condition says that a necessary condition for your knowing that p is that you *believe* that p. In other words, you must think that the proposition is true, or hold that what it says really is the case. This is certainly plausible. After all, it appears that you cannot know something to be true if you don't even believe it. So, for example, it is incoherent to say that you know that it is raining when you don't believe that it is.

None the less, philosophers have disputed the belief condition by arguing that knowledge and belief are *separable* so that each can exist either with or without the other. Some philosophers have even claimed that the two are mutually *incompatible*, or in other words that if you have one you cannot have the other. While Plato in the *Meno* adheres to the view that knowledge entails belief, in a later work, *The Republic*, he develops an incompatibilist view. There he reasons that since knowledge is infallible and belief is fallible, they must be fundamentally different ways of apprehending the world.[65] To believe is to be ambivalent about the object of one's belief. Knowledge involves no such hesitation. So to know something doesn't entail also believing it, but rather involves going *beyond* mere belief. There is no need to discuss Plato's argument in detail here, but one might defend such a position by pointing out that people often speak as if knowledge and belief were distinct, as when tennis players say, 'I don't believe I will win, I *know* I will'. Doesn't this imply that to come to know something is to cease to believe it? In fact it is doubtful that it does, for surely this is just a more emphatic way of saying, 'I don't *just* believe that I will win, I know I will'?

The view that one can have knowledge without belief has also been defended by philosophers who claim that knowledge is more about how one acts than about what beliefs one might entertain. So it is argued, for example, that knowledge is more about responding correctly to questions than it is about any state of mind. If I forget that I have learned the history of some period and am quizzed on it, it might be that I am able to give correct answers but believe them to be mere guesses. Since I am guessing, I seem not to have belief, and yet my getting the answers right suggests I do have knowledge.

Despite this, it would seem that some tendency to assent to a proposition is required of knowledge. Perhaps just choosing an answer, however unsure I may be, is sufficient assent to count as belief. So long as I am disposed to assent to a proposition then I can be said to believe it, and, in this minimal sense, belief certainly seems necessary for knowledge. So it seems that belief is a necessary condition for knowledge and that incompatibilism is wrong.

2 The truth condition

The truth condition is fairly uncontroversial. It says that if you know something it must be true. To test this condition try to think of a case where you knew something that was in fact false. Is this possible? Often we *claim* to know something that turns out to be false, but this doesn't mean that we actually do know it. Thinking you know something is not the same as actually knowing it.

Consider Raquel, a cavewoman living thousands of years ago. She believes that the Earth is flat. She has compelling evidence for this belief. First, it looks flat. Second, if the ground were curved then things would roll off towards the edges and eventually fall off, and so on. Does she know that it is flat? Surely not. If she knows that the Earth is flat, then the Earth must be flat. If it is not flat then Raquel cannot know that it is. Of course, she may well have excellent evidence and be completely convinced and we could understand why she would claim to know, but this by itself is not sufficient for knowledge.

People sometimes talk as if Raquel does have knowledge. They might say that thousands of years ago people knew that the Earth was flat, and now we know that it is round. But when they use the word 'know' in this way they are probably using it as a synonym for 'were convinced'. Strictly speaking, this is not knowledge, but simply a well justified, but false belief. So it seems that the proposition 'S knows that p' entails that p, and it cannot be true if p is false. In other words, you cannot know something if it is false no matter how good the justification for your belief may be.

One important point to draw from this is that whether or not a person knows something cannot be established by *internal* criteria alone (meaning internal to their mind). Raquel cannot simply inspect her belief to determine whether it counts as knowledge. By examining her mind she can establish that she fulfils two of the conditions for knowledge: she has a belief for which she has good justification. She knows this because these two criteria are internal, they are directly accessible to her, since they are 'in her mind' as it were. But for it to count as knowledge it must also be true. Her belief must actually correspond with reality, and this is an *external* criterion.

■ **Figure 5.2**
Knowledge is impossible without truth

Raquel the cavewoman believes the Earth is flat, but in fact it is round. Since her belief doesn't correspond with the facts it is not true. And if it is not true it cannot count as knowledge. The truth condition is 'external' since, unlike the belief and evidence conditions, it is not 'in her mind'.

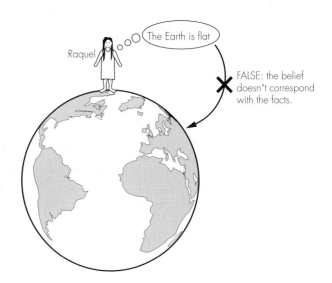

Raquel

The Earth is flat

FALSE: the belief doesn't correspond with the facts.

So a justified, false belief is not knowledge, and truth is considered to be a necessary condition of knowledge.

3 The evidence/justification condition

We have seen Plato argue that we are reluctant to grant someone knowledge if they have acquired a true belief by inadequate evidence, or by sheer luck; and so that we need a third condition. So if S claims to know that p then she must be able to justify it by appeal to evidence, since otherwise she is simply making an unsubstantiated assertion. A good way of illustrating this point is to consider the example of a racist juror. Suppose the juror comes to believe that a defendant is guilty purely on the basis of the colour of his skin. Let's also suppose that, as a matter of fact, the defendant is guilty. In this case, the juror has a true belief. But is it knowledge? It is generally thought that the answer here must be 'no' since the juror has no good justification for her belief. Her belief is based on irrational prejudice, not on the evidence presented to her in court.[66] So an unjustified, true belief is not knowledge.

Are the JTB conditions jointly sufficient?

We have seen why philosophers have felt that each condition is necessary; and hence that you can't do without any one if you want to have knowledge. But if the traditional account of knowledge is right, we must also show that the conditions are jointly sufficient, in other words that if you have all three then you definitely have knowledge. So is justified, true belief sufficient for knowledge?

Belief and subjective certainty

more difficult

Some philosophers have argued that knowledge entails more than merely having a justified, true belief, but also requires feelings of *certainty*. In this view, knowledge doesn't simply require that someone assents to a proposition, but that she possesses a degree of conviction that the proposition is true. The idea here is that if I am not sure of the correct answer to a question, even though I have good evidence for it and give the right answer, then I can't really be said to know it.

Let's consider whether this is correct through an example. Imagine that you are on a famous quiz show on TV and have managed to get through to the last round where you have a chance to win a million pounds. All you have to do is answer the question correctly. However, if you get the answer wrong you risk losing nearly half a million of the winnings you've so far accumulated. So the pressure is on. The question is posed: 'Who wrote the *Meditations on First Philosophy*? Is it a) Des O'Connor, b) Descartes, c) the Dalai Lama, or d) David Beckham?' In such a circumstance, even though you have studied philosophy and have excellent evidence that Descartes is the correct answer, you might experience doubts. Could the book in which you read about Descartes be a hoax? Does

Beckham write philosophy between matches? Is it a trick question? Despite your doubts, you plump for the correct answer: Descartes. So, did you know this was the answer?

If certainty is necessary for knowledge, the answer would be that you didn't. But according to the JTB account of knowledge you did, since, despite your hesitancy, you had a justified, true belief. So which view is correct? It is clear that doubts can creep in even when we have good evidence for beliefs that are true. In such cases, we will not claim to have knowledge, and this is the reason why they seem not to be cases of knowledge. However, the JTB account says that someone's reluctance to claim to know doesn't necessarily show that they don't know. In the example of the quiz programme, it may simply be that you are a very sceptical and diffident person. You may be particularly afraid of making a fool of yourself on national television. But such psychological facts about you don't warrant the conclusion that you don't have knowledge.

This is perhaps clearer if we imagine another contestant in the same situation as you who has none of your worries. They are naturally confident and always think they are right. They have exactly the same evidence as you that Descartes wrote the *Meditations*, having read the same book on the subject. Do they have knowledge? Presumably they do. But if they do then surely you do too, since the only difference lies in the degree of conviction you have in your beliefs. So the conclusion appears to be that facts about *subjective* certainty, that is about how confident one is of the truth of one's beliefs, do not have any bearing on whether or not one knows. It would seem that justified, true belief is sufficient for knowledge, even when the believer may have no conviction in his or her belief.

This observation requires us to draw an important distinction: that between the kind of certainty that is applicable to *people* and that which is applicable to *propositions*. For example, many people would say that they are certain that God exists while few would say that the proposition 'God exists' is certain. To say, 'p is certain' is different from saying 'S is certain that p'. We can use the terms 'objective' and 'subjective' to denote these two sorts of certainty. So while you and the other contestant may differ in the degree of subjective certainty you have in your belief that Descartes wrote the *Meditations*, the certainty of the proposition that he did has equal objective support. What we have argued here is that subjective certainty is not important for knowledge.

Certainty as sufficient

more difficult

Although these considerations suggest that subjective certainty is not *necessary* for knowledge, some philosophers have none the less maintained that it is *sufficient* for at least some basic beliefs. They claim that absolute certainty by itself establishes that one has knowledge and so eliminates the need for further justification. The argument goes that if one is absolutely certain, then there is no possibility of error and so knowledge is guaranteed. Certainty would then do away with the need for the evidence condition for some beliefs. We saw earlier that Descartes talks this way about certain basic beliefs that can be said to be self-justifying and so do not require further evidence: his 'clear and distinct ideas'.

However, if any beliefs can be known in this way, it is surely not simply because of the subjective certainty that the knower may feel about them. Subjective certainty cannot be a sufficient condition for knowledge – after all, many politicians are convinced their policies are the right ones, but few of us would say that they knew them to be. The gambler we discussed earlier may be convinced he will win, but this doesn't mean that he knows he will. So what makes basic beliefs known must be their objective certainty. That 2 + 3 = 5 may be knowable without further justification, since it is objectively certain, but not because I or you happen to be convinced it is true. As we saw in our discussion of the truth condition, this shows that I cannot determine whether I know something simply by inspecting my belief. Internal criteria are not sufficient for knowledge. The belief must also be objectively true, and this condition (the truth condition) is external.

Having said this, we should note an important exception, namely when the belief in question is about one's own mind. For example, if I believe I have a headache or am experiencing a pleasant taste, the thing believed is in my own mind. In these cases, all three JTB conditions can be internally established and so such knowledge (knowledge of one's own mental state) appears knowable just by introspecting – there can be no room for doubt. As we've seen, both Descartes and Locke recognised that there appears to be a special kind of certainty attending to such beliefs since there are no external facts with which the internal belief needs to match up. Without a gap between the belief and an external reality, there is no space for the sceptic to exploit, and this is why such beliefs were thought to be incorrigible.

Knowing that one knows

These observations about subjective certainty lead us on to another important point to consider about knowledge. They suggest that having knowledge doesn't imply knowing that one has knowledge. In other words, it is quite possible for me to know, without knowing that I know. For example, we are inclined to attribute knowledge to people who answer questions correctly in exams, even if they have no confidence in their responses. We are inclined to confer knowledge on ourselves about who wrote the *Meditations* despite our doubts. This suggests that knowledge has more to do with a person's dispositions to behave in certain ways, such as to respond correctly to questions, and less about their state of mind.

To understand this point, consider again the case of the cavewoman Raquel. She thinks she knows that the Earth is flat, but in fact it is round. Having decided that this suggests that she doesn't know it is flat, it is natural to begin thinking of our own position. These days most people reckon the Earth is round, and, like Raquel, we have excellent evidence for this conviction. But it is conceivable that we are mistaken. Perhaps scientists in the future will discover that the earth is flat after all. And if it is flat, then we don't now know that it is round. Does this mean that we don't now know that it is round? No, it just means that if it is flat we don't now know, but if it is round we do know. So the fact that it is conceivable that we don't actually now know that it is round doesn't mean that we don't know that it is round. If it is round we know, and if it is flat we don't. This means we can know that it is round, without having to know that we know it.

In fact, this conclusion can be reached by another argument. If we needed to know that we knew something before we could know it, then presumably we would also need to know that we knew that we knew something before we could know that we knew it. But clearly this quickly generates an infinite regress. Whenever we know something we would also have to know a million and one other things, namely not just that we know it, but that we know that we know it, that we know that we know that we know it, and so on. In other words, if we reckon we have to know that we know in order to know, then 'S knows that p' implies that S knows that (S knows that p). And S knows that (S knows that p) implies that S knows that [S knows that (S knows that p)]; which in turn implies that S knows that (S knows that [S knows that (S knows that p)]). The need for such an infinite regress seems absurd. It would make knowledge impossible, and so we can conclude that we don't need to know that we know something to know it.

■ Figure 5.3
Knowledge is
possible without
knowing you know

As in Figure 5.2, Raquel
cannot know that the Earth
is flat despite good
evidence, because it isn't.
So what of our case? Our
case looks rather similar
since we have good
evidence that the Earth
is round, but it is
conceivable that we are
mistaken. Does this mean
we can't know either?
Not according to the JTB
account. So long as we
have a justified belief that
is true, i.e. which
corresponds with the facts,
then we have knowledge.
We may not know
whether our belief does
correspond with the facts,
but if it does then we do
indeed know.

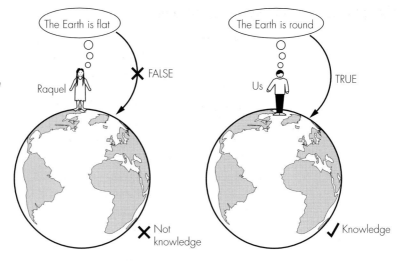

We have argued so far that belief, truth and justification are
all necessary for knowledge. Having done so it would seem
that we are well on the way to establishing that they are
jointly sufficient as well. If they are, then having a justified,
true belief guarantees that you have knowledge. However, we
can't be too hasty. One philosopher famously argued that it
was possible to have a justified, true belief but still not have a
case of knowledge. If he is right, then there is more to
knowing than having justified, true beliefs.

Gettier-type objections to the traditional analysis

► criticism ◄   In 1967 Edmund Gettier (1927–) published a short paper
entitled 'Is Justified, True Belief Knowledge?' It purported to
give examples of *beliefs* which are both *true* and apparently
justified but which we are inclined not to count as examples
of *knowledge*.[67] In other words, while accepting that the three
conditions are individually necessary, he questioned whether
they were jointly sufficient. If he had indeed discovered such
counter-examples then this would show that the three
conditions were not sufficient for knowledge. The examples
he and others have subsequently used have become known as
Gettier counter-examples. Look at the examples on the next
page. Do they raise doubt on the justified, true belief account
of knowledge?

experimenting with ideas

Consider the Gettier-style counter-examples below. Then answer the following questions.

1 Do you think the person in each of the examples has knowledge?
2 Do you think the person has a justified, true belief?
3 Do you think these examples mean that having a justified, true belief is not the same thing as having knowledge?
4 Can you come up with your own Gettier-style counter-example showing a case of a justified, true belief that we are unlikely to accept as a case of knowing?

Example 1

Imagine that one evening you watch a nature programme and you hear David Attenborough say that the killer whale is the fastest swimming sea mammal. As a consequence you acquire the belief that the killer whale is the fastest sea mammal. As a matter of fact this belief is true: killer whales are indeed the fastest of all sea mammals. Moreover it is justified since David Attenborough is a reliable source of information about wildlife. So here is a clear-cut case of a justified, true belief. However, unremarked by you, the evening in question was that of 1 April, and the nature programme was a spoof littered with amusing falsehoods about the natural world. Given this extra fact, could you still be said to know that the killer whale is the fastest sea mammal?

Example 2

Imagine you ride into town at around noon and look up at the clock tower to check the time. The clock says 12 o'clock and so you come to believe that it is 12 o'clock. In fact it is 12 o'clock. Checking a clock is an excellent justification for your belief and so we have here an example of justified, true belief. However, unbeknown to you, the clock has in fact stopped. And the fact that it was telling the correct time at precisely the moment when you chanced to look up at it is a remarkable coincidence. Can you be said to know at that moment that it is 12 o'clock?

Example 3

Jonathan comes home from work early in order to watch the world triple jump championships. He doesn't know it but the BBC are having technical difficulties with their broadcast, so to keep the viewers happy they show a replay of the triple jump final from four years ago, and in the mayhem forget to put on the symbol that shows it to be a repeat. Jonathan switches on the TV and is excited to see Richard Long win the event with a jump of 18.27 metres. Naturally he does not realise this was a replay. As it happens, whilst the replay was being shown, Richard Long did actually win this year's triple jump, remarkably with a jump of 18.27 metres. Does John know that Richard Long won the triple jump?

In cases like these, while people have a *true belief* that seems to be reasonably *justified* and so all three conditions have been met, many would argue that the people do not have *knowledge*. This seems to throw doubt on the idea that knowledge is simply justified, true belief. How are we to react to such problem cases?

Reactions to Gettier

Initially perhaps the most attractive response is to defend the traditional account by arguing that the reason that we are reluctant to say that these people have knowledge is simply that their beliefs are not justified in the proper way. So the idea would be that we need to define our notion of justification more strictly so as to rule out these counter-examples. For example, we ought not to trust the BBC since it is always possible that the programme makers are pulling our legs or running the wrong footage. And we ought not to trust clocks since they may have stopped.

However, this line of argument faces two opposing problems. On the one hand, it is difficult to see how one could define '*proper* justification' in such a way as to prevent Gettier-type examples arising. So, while we might be inclined to say that one is only justified in believing what the BBC say about wildlife if one has first checked the date, or cross-referenced what they say against an encyclopedia, it would seem that further Gettier-type scenarios can always be dreamt up. One could be deceived about the date, the encyclopedia might contain a misprint, and so on.

But on the other hand, even if we did succeed in defining 'proper justification' in such a strict way as to eliminate the possibility of error, this creates another problem. A method of acquiring beliefs that could avoid the risk of ever going wrong in cases like Gettier's would be terribly strict, and even infallible. This would involve us in saying that we don't really know the things we think we know and this entails a radical redefinition of our ordinary concept of knowledge. So, for example, we could no longer rely on the testimony of others since it is always possible that they are mistaken or have reason to lie. We would have to say that I don't really know most of what I think I know about the natural world, since I have learned a lot of it from unreliable sources such as the BBC. And, it would seem that I can hardly ever be said to know the time since I acquire my beliefs about the time almost exclusively by checking a single watch or clock.

Now this may not be a problem. It may be that our common definition of knowledge needs such radical revision. This is certainly the approach that many philosophers have taken. However, it is worth noting that many contemporary philosophers are reluctant to follow them into such a radical redefinition of our ordinary view of what counts as knowledge. To diverge too radically from common usage, they argue, involves us in leaving behind the concept we set out to analyse. Only by holding some sort of connection with ordinary usage and our ordinary intuitions can we be said to be analysing the concept of knowledge at all. We should be asking how we know what we know, and so getting clear about what our concept of knowledge actually is. We should not seriously be wondering whether we really know what we commonly suppose we do.

Another plausible suggestion is that the justification is wrong because it involves, or relies upon, false beliefs. So, in the exercise above, in reasoning to the conclusion that killer whales are the fastest sea mammals, that it is midday, or that Long won the triple jump, you have relied upon false beliefs; namely that the nature programme is not a spoof, that the clock has not stopped, and that the broadcast is live. So we might want to define proper justification as a justification that doesn't rely on any false belief.

However, this suggestion also seems too strong. It seems likely that we hold many false beliefs and many of them will play some role in our reasoning processes. In other words, there is a good chance that some belief I hold, which has a role in the inferential processes underlying the belief in question, is false. But we don't want to give up all claim to knowledge that may have some tenuous connection with a false belief.

more difficult

If the three-part analysis of knowledge is not simply amendable by saying that a proposition cannot be inferred from any false belief, perhaps we need to say that genuine knowledge cannot be inferred from any *relevant* false belief. For this strategy to work we would need to define 'relevance', and one suggestion is that a belief counts as relevant if, were we to cease to believe it, our original claim to knowledge would be undermined. So, in the example of the clock above, if you were to cease to believe that the clock was working properly, then you would cease to claim that you knew the time. This means that the belief that the clock is working properly is *relevant* to the belief that it is noon.

This leads us to a possible way of strengthening the evidence condition. The idea here is that a proper justification for a belief should not be susceptible to being undermined by any further evidence. So your belief that it is noon doesn't count as knowledge just because it could be undermined by further evidence were it to come to light, namely that the clock has stopped. In other words, it is not knowledge because there are further facts which, if you came to believe them, would make you give up your claim to know. And if there are no such further facts, then your claim to know is upheld. A belief that is not susceptible to further evidence, and so would never need to be given up, is termed INDEFEASIBLE. Thus we can modify the analysis of knowledge as being an *indefeasibly* justified, true belief.

This definition, however, also has its detractors although, unfortunately, we are unable to pursue these arguments here. If you are interested, Everitt and Fisher delve further into the issues and go on to examine other attempts to provide a complete analysis of knowledge.[68]

Conclusion

In this final chapter we have focused our attention on knowledge itself and attempted to work out what precisely it is. The view that factual knowledge is no more or less than justified, true belief clearly has much to recommend it, but closer analysis has revealed small but none the less significant inadequacies. Since Gettier, philosophers have put a lot of energy into the search for a definition but none has been entirely successful, leading many to suppose that no exact definition is possible. Why should we expect a term like knowledge, which grows from ordinary usage, to have a core meaning? Ordinary language, after all, contains all sorts of vague concepts, which resist logical analysis. Perhaps knowledge is similar to concepts like 'bald' or 'heap', which have no precise definition but have hazy boundaries. But this need not be a problem. In the previous three chapters we were able to discuss knowledge without having a precise definition, suggesting that we can get on and use a concept without needing to uncover the necessary and sufficient conditions for its use.

Key points: Chapter 5

What you need to know about the **concept of knowledge**:

1 There are three sorts of knowledge: practical knowledge, knowledge by acquaintance, and factual knowledge. Factual knowledge is the kind that philosophers are principally concerned to define. The traditional definition is that knowledge is justified, true belief.

2 Plato argues that true belief is inferior to knowledge because the latter is 'tethered' or justified. Having a belief without proper justification cannot count as knowledge even if the belief happens to be true. So justification is a necessary condition for knowledge and if 'S knows that p' then 'S then p' must be justified.

3 Although some philosophers have felt that knowledge and belief are incompatible, there are strong reasons to think that belief is a necessary condition for knowledge. It seems self-contradictory to say that you know what you don't believe. So if 'S knows that p' then 'S must believe that p'.

4 'S knows that p' implies that p is true. In other words, you can't know something that is false – truth is a necessary condition for knowledge.

5 According to the JTB analysis of knowledge, certainty is neither necessary nor sufficient for knowledge. Moreover, someone can know something without knowing that they do.

6 Gettier questions whether the JTB conditions are jointly sufficient for knowledge by giving examples of justified, true beliefs that are not knowledge.

7 One way of meeting Gettier's counter-examples is to shore up the evidence condition so that knowledge is defined as *indefeasibly* justified, true belief. This means that there is no further evidence that could come to light that would undermine the belief.

Conclusion

So what have we learned? By way of conclusion it may be worth reviewing some of the terrain we have covered.

The role of scepticism

We started by examining what we can claim to know and how we can justify these claims. To help in this process philosophers have often used the tool of scepticism. With sceptical arguments they try to identify dubious and unwanted beliefs, to distinguish what we can know from what we cannot know, and to explore just how strong are our justifications for various knowledge claims. If we thought we knew a quite a lot of stuff beforehand, the encounter with scepticism is liable to make us a little more modest. Indeed, the cumulative effect of the several sceptical arguments we looked at is to make it seem that we actually know very little at all, if anything!

In search of certainty

One reaction to this uncomfortable situation is to search for claims that cannot be doubted, thereby showing that scepticism cannot encompass all our beliefs. But the tendency to equate what we can know with what is indubitable or certain still leaves us knowing very little and so can provide us with only limited success against the sceptic. We might hope to rebuild a body of knowledge upon indubitable foundations but, as we have seen, both the rationalist and empiricist efforts to do so encounter serious difficulties. For example, the few indubitable truths Descartes uncovers, namely knowledge of my own existence, of my own sense experiences, and of simple mathematical truths, fail to allay the possibility that a demon may be deceiving me, or that I may be a brain in a vat receiving my sense data from some sort of super computer. Such scenarios raise a genuine concern about how we are to acquire knowledge of an independently existing reality on the basis of our own sensations. Does this mean that we are forced to accept that very little can be known?

No beliefs beyond revision

Perhaps not. Another tack may be to abandon the quest for indubitable foundations for knowledge. Certainty may be something that we aspire to in our knowledge claims, but not something that we often attain. For example, it may be that we should be concerned to adopt beliefs that are useful to us rather than those based on unshakable foundations. Coherentism represents one alternative to the traditional foundationalist approach to epistemology. It argues that the process of justification is about the way a claim fits in with a system of beliefs. By this account, justification becomes a matter of degree rather than an all-or-nothing affair, and no claim within our system of beliefs is totally indubitable and beyond revision. Alternatively, it may be that what is important is the mechanism by which we acquire our beliefs. So long as it is reliable, then it is reasonable to accept them, regardless of whether any explicit justification can be given.

The sources of knowledge

As well as investigating the nature of justification we've considered both rationalist and empiricist accounts of the ultimate sources of our concepts and beliefs. The rationalists searched for it primarily in reason. However, beyond the sphere of mathematics and logic, it seems that reason alone can provide us with few substantive truths. Empiricists argued against the rationalists that all factual knowledge, all knowledge about the world around us, would have to be based on evidence gained from perception. Their project was to build a body of scientific knowledge on the indubitable and indefeasible data of sense. One crucial difficulty concerns whether these data are as secure as the empiricist might hope. Another historically significant problem involves what Kant called the scandal of modern philosophy, namely its failure to establish a proof of the existence of a world beyond our own sensations. The attempts to grapple with this problem formed the core of our discussion of perception in Chapter 4. Can we suppose our sensations to give accurate information about the world? Could it be that it distorts it radically? Indeed, could the world be reduced to our perception of it, and physical objects be nothing more than patterns of sense data?

Defining 'knowledge'

One tactic we've looked at for resisting scepticism is to argue that the sceptic may misunderstand what 'knowledge' actually is. The philosopher may be searching for an ideal of knowledge that is impossible to attain. But if we clarify what knowledge really is, we may find that it is within our grasp after all. The final chapter attempted to home in on a definition in order to clarify for what we are actually looking. In the process, we began to see the enormous difficulties that attend efforts to pin down what knowledge is, and although we were unable to pursue the investigation further, it may well be that no completely satisfactory analysis of this concept can be found.

In the five thousand years since the advent of writing there has been a huge explosion in the extent of human knowledge. The invention of the printing press and latterly the internet have fuelled the advance of science and of our capacity to understand the universe. Yet despite these developments, giving a clear account of knowledge and of the relationship between our beliefs and the world remains as difficult as it has ever been.

Glossary

Analytic and synthetic   An analytic proposition is true by definition, or simply because of the meanings of the terms used to express it. Kant, who first introduced the term, explained the idea by saying that an analytic statement is one of subject–predicate form where the predicate is 'contained within' or is part of the meaning of the subject. For example, in the statement 'Bachelors are single' the term 'bachelors' is the subject and 'are single' is the predicate, and the latter is 'contained within' the former. This means that by analysing the concept of the subject one can see that the concept of the predicate is contained within it. A synthetic proposition is one where the predicate is not contained within the subject, or where its truth cannot be determined simply by analysing the meanings of the terms used. For example, 'Bachelors are miserable'.

Anti-realism   If you are a *realist* about something, then you believe it exists independently of our minds. If you are an *anti-realist* about something you think it is mind-dependent. Here the terms are used to describe two approaches to the nature of perception. Realists are those who believe that material objects have an existence independent of our perception of them. Two forms of realism are discussed here: **naïve realism** and **representative realism**. Anti-realists about perception reckon that material objects exist only for minds and that a mind-independent world is non-existent. Berkeley summed up the position by saying that to be is to be perceived. Two forms of anti-realism are discussed here: **idealism** and **phenomenalism**.

A priori/ a posteriori   These terms are Latin for from what comes before or *prior* to and from what comes after or *posterior* to. They refer to two sorts of proposition and how one can come to know them. *A priori* propositions can be known to be true prior to, or independently of, experience. For example, one can know *a priori* that 2 + 3 = 5 since one need only think about the sum to work out

that it is correct. No reference to the world or to one's experience is necessary to recognise its truth. Of course, to see that it is true one does need to understand the meanings of the terms it uses and these meanings are learned through experience. But what makes such knowledge *a priori* is that it does not depend on experience for its justification. By contrast, *a posteriori* knowledge depends upon evidence that can only be gained through experience. To know that it is a sunny day, one has to look out of the window, ask a friend, or some such. We cannot work it out just by thinking about it.

Argument   An argument is a series of propositions intended to support a conclusion. The propositions offered in support of the conclusion are termed *premises*.

Belief   A belief is a state of mind or thought about the world. It is a mental representation which claims that something is the case, or that a proposition is true. For example, you may have the belief that cod liver oil is good for health. A belief will have some degree of evidence in support of it but is normally regarded as weaker than knowledge, either because knowledge cannot turn out to be false, or because it requires stronger evidence.

Clear and distinct ideas   The basic or self-justifying beliefs that Descartes hopes to use as foundations for his system of knowledge. Clear and distinct ideas, we are told, are those which can be 'intuited' by the mind by what he calls the 'light of reason'. In other words, they are truths of *reason*, truths that can be known with the mind alone. Descartes' examples of clear and distinct ideas are the basic claims of logic, geometry and mathematics. Knowledge of truths of reason, it is claimed, resists any sceptical attack, since we recognise their truth immediately. Our faculty of 'intuition' permits us to recognise their truth without allowing any room for doubt or error. For example, it is in vain to ask how I know that triangles have three sides. Such knowledge is given in the very act of understanding the terms involved. There is no further evidence I need appeal to in order to justify such knowledge.

Cogito   Latin for 'I think', and shorthand for Descartes' famous argument to prove his own existence. Descartes attempted to doubt that he existed, but realised that in order to doubt this, he must exist. So his own existence was indubitable.

Coherentism   The view about the structure of justification that claims that no beliefs are foundational and therefore that all beliefs need justification in terms of further beliefs. By this account, beliefs are more or less justified to the extent that they fit in or cohere with other beliefs in the system.

Concept   Having a concept of something is what enables one to recognise it, distinguish it from other things and think about it. So, if I have the concept of a hedgehog, I can think about hedgehogs, and recognise them when I encounter them, and tell the difference between them and hogs or hedges. Similarly, to have a concept of red is to be able to think about it, recognise it and to distinguish it from other colours. According to traditional empiricism, all our concepts are formed as kinds of 'copy' of the original sensations.

Contingent   A contingent truth is one that happens to be true, but which might not have been. In other words, it is a truth for which it is logically possible that it be false. The opposite of a contingent truth is a necessary one, i.e. one which has to be true and couldn't be otherwise, or for which it is logically impossible that it be false. For example, it is a contingent truth that daffodils are yellow, since it is conceivable that they might have been blue. Propositions are also termed 'contingent' if they may be true or may be false.

Direct realism   Another term for **naïve realism**.

Dualism   Dualism about mind and body is the claim that humans are made of two distinct kinds of stuff – a material body and a spiritual mind.

Empiricism   Those philosophers who argue that most of what we claim to know we must first have had experience of are called

empiricists. Empiricism holds that knowledge claims must be justified by appeal to perception. Empiricism is normally contrasted with rationalism, which claims that most important knowledge is acquired through the application of reason.

Epistemology   The theory of knowledge. A term derived from the Ancient Greek words *episteme* meaning 'knowledge' and *logos* meaning 'account' or 'rationale'.

Evidence   The reasons for holding a belief.

Evil demon   A device used by Descartes to generate a sceptical argument about the possibility of knowledge of the external world and of basic propositions of arithmetic and geometry. It is conceivable that there exists an extremely powerful spirit or demon bent on deceiving me. If this were the case, then all my perception of the world around me could be an illusion produced in my mind by the demon. Even my own body could be a part of the illusion. Moreover, the demon could cause me to make mistakes even about the most simple judgements of maths and geometry so that I go wrong when adding 2 to 3 or counting the sides of a square. See *Meditation 1*.

External world   All that exists outside of or independently of the mind; the physical world.

Fact   Something which is the case. For example, it is a fact that the Earth revolves around the sun.

False   A term used of beliefs and propositions. A false belief is one that is not true. One account of what makes a belief or proposition false is that it fails to correspond with the facts. So, for example, the belief that humans are descended from apes will be false if in fact they are descended from dolphins.

Forms (theory of)   Plato's theory of forms is a theory about types or classes of thing. The word 'form' is used to translate Plato's use of the Greek word 'idea' with which he refers to the type or class to which a thing belongs. Plato argues that over and above the realm of physical objects there is a realm of 'forms' to which the individual physical things belong. So, in the physical realm there are many tables, but there is also the single form of the table, the ideal or blueprint of the table, which we recognise not with our senses, but with the mind.

Foundationalism   The view about the structure of justification that claims that there are two sorts of belief: those which are basic or foundational and which require no justification (or which are self-justifying), and those which are built on top of the foundations and justified in terms of them.

Given   The given is the raw and immediate element of experience prior to any judgement. What is given to us immediately is often termed sense data and such experience is thought to be known for certain and incorrigibly.

Hypothetical statements   'If . . . then' statements which make claims about states of affairs that are not actual, but which would be *if* certain conditions were satisfied. Hypothetical statements are used to translate physical object language into phenomenal language in linguistic phenomenalism.

Idea   The uses of the word 'idea' are various within philosophical literature, as well as in ordinary parlance. Here the word is not used in a technical or precise sense.

Idealism   Idealism as discussed here is an anti-realist theory of perception. Put forward by Berkeley, it is the view that matter does not exist independently of the mind and that all that exists are minds and their ideas. Physical objects are no more than collections of sensations appearing in minds. Objects that are not currently being perceived by any creature are sustained in existence by being perceived in the mind of God.

Incorrigibility   To call a belief incorrigible is to say that it cannot be corrected or changed. Someone who honestly holds a belief that is incorrigible cannot be mistaken about it. Beliefs about our own sense data are often thought to be incorrigible since there appears to be no way in which I can be mistaken about my own experiences and there appears to be no further evidence that could be brought to bear to make me change my mind about what I'm experiencing. For this reason such beliefs are often taken to be immune to sceptical attack.

Indefeasible   The justification for a belief is indefeasible if there is no further evidence that could undermine it and so lead one to give up the belief. By contrast, a justification for a belief is defeasible if there are facts which, if they were to come to light, would count against the belief.

Indirect realism   Another term for **representative realism**. The view that the immediate objects of perception are sense data or representations and that the physical world is perceived only indirectly via these representations.

Indubitable   Not doubtable. A belief that it is not possible to doubt is indubitable.

Induction   The process of reasoning from the particular to the general.

Inference   The move in an argument from the premises or reasons to the conclusion. For example, in the argument 'Moriarty had blood on his hands, therefore he must be the murderer' the inference is the move made from the premise that Moriarty had blood on his hands to the conclusion that he is the murderer.

Innate ideas or knowledge   Ideas that exist in the mind that are not acquired from experience. Plato, for example, argued that all ideas or concepts are innate and that the process of acquiring knowledge is not one of learning in the strict sense, but rather of recollecting what we already implicitly know. So we are all born with innate knowledge of the 'forms' and it is this knowledge that enables us to recognise individual exemplars of the forms in this life. Rationalists traditionally favoured the belief that we possess such ideas. Leibniz, for example, argued that such ideas exist implicitly within the mind and that they are brought to the surface of consciousness through experience. Rationalists often use the doctrine of innate ideas to explain the possibility of *a priori* knowledge. Descartes argued that knowledge of mathematics is innate and that the discovery of mathematical truths involves the mind looking into itself to uncover them. Knowledge of the existence of God is also possible, according to Descartes, because we can look into our own mind to discover the idea and deduce his existence in an *a priori* manner simply through careful mental scrutiny of the idea. Opposed to the doctrine of innate ideas are the empiricists and, in particular, John Locke who devoted the first book of his *Essay Concerning Human Understanding* to their repudiation. Locke argued that all the contents of the mind can be reduced to sensation variously transformed and that the mind at birth is akin to a blank sheet of paper.

Intuition   A kind of mental seeing by which rational truths can be recognised. For Descartes the mind deploys the faculty of intuition when it sees by the 'light of reason' that 2 + 2 = 4 or that a sphere is bounded by one surface.

Justification   The support or grounds for holding a belief, which gives someone a reason for believing it or makes them justified in believing it. The process of justifying a belief is by offering evidence. The traditional analysis of knowledge sees justification as necessary for knowledge.

Knowledge   There are three sorts of knowledge: practical knowledge, knowledge by acquaintance, and factual knowledge. The traditional account of factual knowledge claims that it is justified, true belief.

Materialism   The view that everything in the world is made of matter and that ultimately all mental or apparently spiritual entities can be given a purely material explanation.

Method of doubt   Descartes' sceptical method used to find certainty. Descartes found that many of his beliefs had turned out to be false, and to remedy this situation elected to cast doubt upon all his beliefs. If any beliefs showed themselves to be indubitable, and could survive the most radical scepticism, then they would have established themselves as absolutely certain. Once he had discovered such beliefs, Descartes hoped to rebuild a body of knowledge based on them which would be free from error.

Mitigated scepticism   Hume's expression meaning literally 'moderated' scepticism. Hume argued that radical scepticism in the manner of Descartes could lead only to a dead end in which nothing could be known. To be of any practical use to the philosopher, therefore, scepticism should be used more moderately so as not to destroy one's belief system completely. Scepticism is useful when it is used to reject beliefs which it is unreasonable to hold, but not when used indiscriminately to destroy all one's beliefs.

Naïve realism   The common-sense view of how perception works. Physical objects have an independent existence in space, they follow the laws of physics and possess certain properties, ranging from size and shape through to colour, smell and texture. When humans are in the presence of such objects under appropriate conditions they are able to perceive them along with all these properties.

Necessary   A necessary truth is one which has to be true and couldn't be otherwise, or for which it is logically impossible that it be false.

Necessary and sufficient conditions   A is a *necessary* condition for B when you have to have A in order to have B. In other words, if you don't have A you can't have B. By contrast, A is a *sufficient* condition for B when if you have A you must have B too. In other words, having A is enough or sufficient to guarantee that you have B. When trying to give a logical analysis of the concept of knowledge philosophers have traditionally argued that there are three necessary conditions: you must have a belief, the belief must be true, and it must be justified. To say that each of these is necessary is to say that you need each one or that if you are missing any one then you can't have knowledge. These three conditions are also said to be sufficient for knowledge, meaning that if you have all three then you definitely have knowledge.

Ontology   The study of being in general or of what there is.

Ordinary language philosophy   Ordinary language doesn't have all the fine distinctions or precise meanings that are often necessary in philosophical argument. For this reason, philosophical discourse is often conducted in a language which is very different from that of ordinary life. However, this departure from ordinary discourse brings with it its own problems. By using words in their own peculiar way, philosophers can often create unnecessary bewilderment and confusion. According to ordinary language philosophers, by paying attention to the way terms are ordinarily used some, if not all, philosophical puzzles can be dissolved.

Perception   The process by which we become aware of physical objects, including our own body.

Phenomenalism   An anti-realist theory of perception distinguished from idealism in that it claims that physical objects are collections not just of actual but also of potential sense data. Physical objects continue to exist unperceived since they retain the potential to be perceived.

Primary and secondary qualities   According to representative realism, physical objects have certain primary qualities such as size and shape, which we are able to perceive. At the same time, we also seem to perceive objects to have a set of secondary qualities such as colours, sounds and smells. However, these qualities are not actually in the objects themselves, but rather are powers to produce these sensations in us. Such powers are a product of the arrangement of the parts of the object, which are too small for us to observe.

Proposition   What a statement says or asserts about the world. Like beliefs, propositions can be true or false. So, when someone utters the sentence 'The cat is on the mat' they are expressing the proposition that the cat is on the mat.

Propositional content   The thought expressed by a proposition. A proposition or belief has propositional content if it expresses some thought or proposition. Many linguistic expressions may fail to express a proposition and so have no propositional content – for example, expletives, warnings or expressions of attitude.

Pyrrhonism   Extreme scepticism. Named after Pyrrho (fourth to third century BC), a sceptical philosopher, who maintained that there is always as much evidence against as for any belief, and that it is therefore sensible not to commit oneself to any positive belief.

Rationalism   The tendency in philosophy to regard reason, as opposed to sense experience, as the primary source of the important knowledge of which we are capable. Rationalists are typically impressed by the systematic nature of mathematical knowledge and the possibility of certainty that it affords. Using mathematics as the ideal of how knowledge should be, rationalists typically attempt to extend this type of knowledge into other areas of human enquiry, such as to knowledge of the physical world, or to ethics. Rationalism is traditionally contrasted with empiricism: the view that most of what we know is acquired through experience.

Realism   If you are a *realist* about something, then you believe it exists independently of our minds. If you are an *anti-realist* about something you think it is mind-dependent. Two realist theories of perception are discussed here, namely **naïve realism** and **representative realism**. They have in common the conviction that physical objects are real, that is, that they have an existence independent of our perception of them.

Reason   The capacity for rational argument and judgement. The process by which we are able to discover the truth of things by pure thought, by inferring conclusions from premises. Often contrasted with instinct, emotion or imagination.

Reliabilism   The view of justification that claims that a belief is justified if it is produced by a reliable method rather than by being based on good reasons. A reliable method is one which is most likely to produce a true belief.

Representation   In the philosophy of perception, a representation is a sense experience or collection of sense data which appears to picture some aspect of the physical world, such as an object. (See **representative realism**)

Representative realism   A realist theory of perception which claims that physical objects impact upon our sense organs causing us to experience sensations. These sensations are akin to pictures, which represent the objects that cause them.

Scepticism   Philosophical scepticism entails raising doubts about our claims to know. Global scepticism directs its doubts at all knowledge claims and argues that we can know nothing. Scepticism can also have a more limited application to some subset of our knowledge claims – for example, concerning the possibility of knowledge of the claims of religion or of ethics. The purpose of scepticism in philosophy is firstly to test our knowledge claims. If they can survive the sceptic's attack, then they may vindicate themselves as genuine knowledge. Descartes used scepticism in this way so that he could isolate a few certainties that he felt could be used as a foundation to rebuild a body of knowledge free from doubt or error. Scepticism is also used as a tool for distinguishing which types of belief can be treated as known and which cannot, thereby delimiting those areas where knowledge is possible. In this way philosophers often exclude certain regions of human enquiry as fruitless since they cannot lead to knowledge. Empiricists, for example, often argue that knowledge of religious claims is impossible since they cannot be verified in terms of experience.

Sensation   The subjective experience we have as a consequence of perceiving physical objects including our own bodies, such as the experience of smelling a rose, or of feeling hungry.

Sense data   What one is directly aware of in perception; the subjective elements that constitute experience. For example, when perceiving a banana, what I actually sense is a collection of sense data, the way the banana seems to me, including a distinctive smell, a crescent-shaped yellow expanse, a certain texture and taste. According to sense data theorists, we make judgements about the nature of the physical world on the basis of immediate awareness of these sense data. So, on the basis of my awareness of the sense datum of a yellow expanse, plus that of a banana smell and so on, I judge that I am in the presence of a banana. In this way, we build up a picture of the physical world and so all empirical knowledge can rest on the foundation of sense data.

Solipsism   The view that all that can be known to exist is my own mind. This is not normally a position defended by philosophers, but rather a sceptical trap into which certain ways of thinking appear to lead. For example, if it is urged that all that can be truly known is what one is directly aware of oneself, then it follows that one *cannot* know anything of which one is *not* directly aware. This might include the minds of other people (which one can learn about only via their behaviour), or, more radically, the very existence of the physical world, including one's own body (which one can learn about only via one's sense experience of it).

Superstructural beliefs   The superstructure of a building is the part that rests on the foundations. According to foundationalism our beliefs fall into two categories – the foundational ones and the superstructural ones. The foundational beliefs justify themselves while the superstructural ones are justified by (rest on) the foundational ones.

Statement   Indicative sentence.

Synthetic   See **analytic and synthetic**

Transcendental   A term coined by Kant to describe a certain form of anti-sceptical argument. A transcendental argument operates by showing that the sceptic must presuppose what she attempts to deny in order for her argument to make sense. For example, to defeat the sceptic's claim that we cannot know that the physical universe exists beyond our own minds we would need to show that the existence of that world is presupposed in the formulation of the sceptical argument itself. How this might be done is discussed in more detail in the text.

True   A term used of beliefs and propositions. There are different theories of what makes a belief or proposition true. For the sake of simplicity, in this book we have been operating with the so-called *correspondence* theory of truth, which says that beliefs and propositions are true when they correspond with the facts, that is, when what they say about the world is the case.

Notes

Chapter 2

1 Compare Morton, A., *Philosophy in Practice: An Introduction to the Main Questions*, Blackwell, 1996, p. 14

2 Descartes, *Meditations on First Philosophy*, in Sutcliffe, F. E. (tr.), *Discourse on Method and the Meditations*, Penguin, 1968

3 As note 2.

4 Hume, D., *Enquiry Concerning Human Understanding*, Oxford University Press, 1999, I, iv, 30

5 For discussion of this point, see the sections in Chapter 5 of this book entitled 'Belief and subjective certainty' and 'Certainty as sufficient' (pp. 139, 141)

6 Descartes, *Meditations on First Philosophy*, in Sutcliffe, F. E. (tr.), *Discourse on Method and the Meditations*, Penguin, 1968, p. 96

7 Descartes, *Meditations on First Philosophy*, in Sutcliffe, F. E. (tr.), *Discourse on Method and the Meditations*, Penguin, 1968, p. 100

8 Descartes, *Meditations on First Philosophy*, in Sutcliffe, F. E. (tr.), *Discourse on Method and the Meditations*, Penguin, 1968, p. 100

9 Descartes, *Principles of Philosophy*, in Haldane, E. S. and Ross, G. R. T. (tr.s), *The Philosophical Works of Descartes*, Cambridge University Press, 1911, 1, vii

10 Descartes, *Meditations on First Philosophy*, in Sutcliffe, F. E. (tr.), *Discourse on Method and the Meditations*, Penguin, 1968, p. 103

11 For example, this criticism is made by Hume, D. in *A Treatise on Human Nature* (I, iv, 6) and Wittgenstein, L. in *Tractatus Logico-Philosophicus*, Routledge, 1974 (5.621–5.6331)

12 A similar argument can be made against the sceptical claim that we may always be dreaming since when dreaming we can't tell if we are awake or not. It makes no sense to suppose that one could be dreaming *all* the time since the concept of dreaming is in part determined by that of being awake.

13 Descartes, *Discourse on Method*, in Lafleur, L. J. (tr.), *Philosophical Essays*, Bobbs-Merrill, 1964, p. 18

14 Pyrrho (fourth to third century BC), a sceptical philosopher, maintained that there is always as much evidence against as for any belief, and that it is therefore sensible not to commit oneself to any positive belief. When he flinched from a vicious dog, thereby revealing at least that he believed it might hurt him, he is said to have conceded that it is hard to escape one's human nature. Like Hume, then, he recognised that we are limited in what we can suspend judgement about in the practice of living.

15 Hume, D., *Enquiry Concerning Human Understanding*, Oxford University Press, 1999, I, xii, 126

16 Hume, D., *Enquiry Concerning Human Understanding*, Oxford University Press, 1999, I, xii, 126–9

17 Moore, G. E., 'A Defence of Common Sense' in *Philosophical Papers*, Muirhead Library of Philosophy, 1959

18 Reid, T., *An Inquiry into the Human Mind, on the Principles of Common Sense*, in *The Works of Thomas Reid*, Machlachlan, Stuart & Co., 1846, p. 127

Chapter 3

19 It is worth reminding ourselves that at one point in *Meditation 1* Descartes raises doubts even about the seemingly self-evident truths of mathematics and geometry. He asks whether he can be certain that a square has four sides or that $2 + 3 = 5$ since it is possible to make mistakes and so an all-powerful demon could make him go wrong here as well. This use of the method of doubt raises important questions discussed above in the section entitled 'Hume's mitigated scepticism' (p. 31). The issue turns on whether raising such radical doubts undermines Descartes' whole enterprise. If he begins to doubt his own reasoning processes, then surely he can no longer trust that he is making cogent arguments and would have to give up philosophising. This shows that a certain minimal amount of trust is required in order for one to conduct any enquiry.

20 For a good account of this distinction, see Everitt, N. and Fisher, A., *Modern Epistemology: A New Introduction*, McGraw Hill Inc., 1995, pp. 72–73

21 Plato, *Meno*, Penguin, 1956, pp. 82–85

22 Plato, *The Republic*, Penguin, 1955, 485b

23 For example, Plato, *The Republic*, Penguin, 1955, 475d–476d

24 Of course, this is not to say that mathematics is of no *use*. We may well be able to apply mathematics to the physical world to explain and predict things.

25 Leibniz's view that we live in the best possible world has caused a fair amount of controversy and it was savagely satirised by the French writer Voltaire (1694–1778) in his novel *Candide.*

26 Note that this position raises difficulties for our ordinary, common-sense view that in all kinds of situations we could do otherwise than we actually did. In other words, it seems to deny that we have free will. Both Leibniz and Spinoza are aware of this apparent implication and have complex and ingenious ways of dealing with it, which we have no space to go into here.

27 Discussion of their (ontological) argument and the various objections that can be made to it can be found in the companion books published in this series – *Philosophy of Religion* and *Descartes'* Meditations.

28 For an example of this view, see Hume, D., *Enquiry Concerning Human Understanding*, Oxford University Press, 1999, I, ii

29 Descartes, *Meditations on First Philosophy*, in Sutcliffe, F. E. (tr.), *Discourse on Method and the Meditations*, Penguin, 1968, p. 107, our emphasis

30 Locke, J., *An Essay Concerning Human Understanding* (1690), Dent and Sons, 1961, II, 1, 3

31 Hume, D., *Enquiry Concerning Human Understanding*, Oxford University Press, 1999, I, iv

32 For a discussion of Descartes' argument to this effect, see the companion book in this series, *Descartes'* Meditations, and the discussion of wax in *Meditation 3.*

33 See p. 142 for the distinction between *knowing how* and *knowing that.*

34 This is a problem to which we will be returning in detail when we look at the philosophy of perception in Chapter 4.

35 As John Stuart Mill argues in Mill, J. S., *System of Logic* (1843), in Robson, F. M. (ed.), *Collected Works of J. S. Mill*, vol. vii, Routledge & Kegan Paul, 1973

36 Kant, I., *The Critique of Pure Reason* (1781), Macmillan, 1929, A51, B75

37 These examples are from Chalmers, A. F., *What is this thing called Science?*, Open University Press, 1987, pp. 243–315

38 This may appear to be an extraordinary conclusion. Could we really be brought to give up the idea that all vixens are foxes, or that 2 + 2 = 4? For a discussion of this possibility, see Morton, A., *A Guide through the Theory of Knowledge* second edition, Blackwell, 1977, pp. 57–58, and Everitt, N. and Fisher, A., *Modern Epistemology: A New Introduction*, McGraw Hill Inc., 1995, Chapter 7.5 and Logic Appendix 6.

39 See note 38.

Chapter 4

40 Hume, D., *Enquiry Concerning Human Understanding*, Oxford University Press, 1999, I, xii, 118

41 Berkeley, G., *First Dialogue* in *Three Dialogues* in *A New Theory of Vision and Other Writings*, Everyman, 1963, p. 214

42 Berkeley, G., *First Dialogue* in *Three Dialogues* in *A New Theory of Vision and Other Writings*, Everyman, 1963, p. 208

43 Locke, J., *An Essay Concerning Human Understanding*, Oxford University Press, 1999, Book II, ch. 8

44 For those studying dualism, Descartes uses this argument to establish the nature of matter and mind/spirit (Descartes, *Meditations on First Philosophy*, in Sutcliffe, F. E. (tr.), *Discourse on Method and the Meditations*, Penguin, 1968, *Meditation 6*, p. 156). He claims that extension (occupying space) is the only property we can't conceive matter without. So that must be its essential feature. And the one thing you can't conceive a mind without is thought, so thought is the essential property of mind. Some philosophers, however, have criticised this whole method of establishing essential and non-essential properties. It seems to rely on what humans can and cannot imagine, and this would seem to introduce a subjective element into the proceedings. For example, perhaps matter can exist without extension – but humans simply can't conceive of it as such.

45 While our perception of secondary qualities may be a kind of illusion, it is not without its function. Matter itself may not be coloured in

the sense that my experience of red is out there on the surfaces of things. But an apple does have certain properties that we succeed in picking out by seeing it as red, and it is often useful to us to be able to recognise these properties. For example, the ability to see red helps us pick out ripe fruits from a leafy background. Similarly with tastes – food stuffs may not be objectively bitter, but foods that taste bitter to us may often be poisonous.

46 Locke, J., *An Essay Concerning Human Understanding* (1690), Dent and Sons, 1961, II, viii, 10

47 Immanuel Kant (1724–1804) argued along these lines in his revolutionary work *The Critique of Pure Reason* (1781). Kant's big idea was that we should give up being concerned with trying to prove that the way we perceive and understand the world conforms to reality (world one), since this is impossible. Instead he tried to demonstrate that the only 'reality' we can know is the one which conforms to our perception and understanding, i.e. world two. Since all objects of experience must, he argued, appear in space and time and are subject to causality, this is the only world we can know. Knowledge is limited to appearances: to world two. Nothing can be known about the real world: world one.

48 A similar problem to this is found in modern-day physics. Physics tries to explain and predict the world we perceive around us, whether occurring in everyday life or through complex experiments. However, it appears that in dealing with entities that we cannot perceive with our eyes, the everyday concepts we use to apply to the world, e.g. motion, causation, wave, particle, no longer apply in a straightforward way. It seems our conceptual language is fine for dealing with the large, everyday objects of perception, but not in dealing with minute atomic and subatomic particles.

49 The meaning of the term 'idea' as used by the empiricists of the eighteenth century is notoriously difficult to pin down. Berkeley's use follows Locke's for whom the term means whatever one is conscious of. So, while including what we are here calling sense data, it would also include beliefs and concepts. Note also that Berkeley's arguments discussed above concerning the distinction between primary and secondary qualities are in fact strategic ones, and his

considered position actually denies that there is any such distinction.

50 A second argument involves showing that if secondary qualities exist only in the mind of the perceiver, then so do primary qualities of figure, extension, motion and solidity. See Berkeley, G., *First Dialogue* in *Three Dialogues* in *A New Theory of Vision and Other Writings*, Everyman, 1963, pp. 218–222.

51 This argument has much in common with the arguments used by Hume discussed in Chapter 3 in the section entitled 'Hume and empiricism' (see p. 62). Hume uses the empiricist claim that all genuine ideas must derive from experience to argue that we don't really have an idea of self, for example.

52 Knox, R., in *The Complete Limerick Book*, Langford Reed, 1924. The second part of the limerick (the answer) is thought to be either by an anonymous author, or by Bertrand Russell (because he uses them in several books).

53 Boswell, J., *Life of Samuel Johnson*, Clarendon Press, 1804, I, p. 471

54 Boswell, J., *Life of Samuel Johnson*, Clarendon Press, 1804, IV, p. 27

55 Moore, G. E., 'Proof of an External World' in *Philosophical Papers*, Muirhead Library of Philosophy, 1959, p. 145

56 Hume, D., *A Treatise on Human Nature*, Oxford University Press, 1978, p. 187

57 Mill, J. S., *Examination of Sir William Hamilton's Philosophy*, in Robson, F. M. (ed.), *Collected Works of J. S. Mill*, vol. ix, Routledge & Kegan Paul, 1979 p. 183

58 Berkeley, G., *Principles of Human Knowledge*, in *A New Theory of Vision and Other Writings*, Everyman, 1963, 3: 58.

Chapter 5

59 It is important to distinguish sentences from the propositions they may be used to express. This is because, on the one hand, different sentences can express the same proposition. For example, consider the two different sentences: 'Romeo loves Juliet' and 'Juliet is loved by Romeo'. Both clearly have the same meaning and assert the same thought. In other words, they express the same proposition. Similarly, sentences in different languages can be used to express the same proposition. 'Je cherche mon chapeau' and 'I'm looking for my hat' are clearly different sentences, but they express the same

proposition. On the other hand, the *same* sentence can be used to express *different* propositions, depending on the context. So the sentence 'I love you' as spoken by Romeo to Juliet expresses the proposition that Romeo loves Juliet, but if spoken by Jack to Jill expresses the proposition that Jack loves Jill. Finally, it is important to note that not all sentences express a proposition. Sentences can also be used to ask questions, to express an attitude, to make an exclamation, issue a command, and so on. What distinguishes propositions from other uses of language is that they can be either true or false. In other words, propositions can be asserted or denied.

60 Plato, *Meno*, Penguin, 1956 (97a–b, translation modified)

61 Plato, *Meno*, Penguin, 1956 (97e–98e)

62 'Well of course, I have only been using an analogy myself, not knowledge.' (Plato, *Meno*, Penguin, 1956, 98b)

63 Plato, *Theaetetus*, Penguin, 1987, 201c–d

64 Plato, *Theaetetus*, Penguin, 1987, 201d

65 Plato, *The Republic*, Penguin, 1955, 476–479

66 An exception to this might be the religious believer who claims to know without any justification, by faith alone.

67 Gettier, E., 'Is Justified, True Belief Knowledge?' in Philips Griffiths, A. (ed.) *Knowledge and Belief*, Oxford University Press, 1967

68 Everitt, N. and Fisher, A., *Modern Epistemology: A New Introduction*, McGraw Hill Inc., 1995, chapters 2 and 3

Selected bibliography

Recommended reading

Audi, Robert, *Epistemology: A Contemporary Introduction to the Theory of Knowledge*, Routledge, 1998

Cole, Peter, *Theory of Knowledge*, Hodder & Stoughton, 2002

Descartes, *Meditations on First Philosophy*, in Sutcliffe, F. E. (tr.), *Discourse on Method and the Meditations*, Penguin, 1968

Everitt, Nicholas and Fisher, Alec, *Modern Epistemology: A New Introduction*, McGraw-Hill Inc., 1995

Hospers, John, *An Introduction to Philosophical Analysis* (second edition), Routledge and Kegan Paul, 1967

Morton, Adam, *A Guide through the Theory of Knowledge* (second edition), Blackwell, 1977

Russell, B., *The Problems of Philosophy*, Oxford University Press, 1912

Trusted, Jennifer, *An Introduction to the Philosophy of Knowledge* (second edition), Palgrave, 1997

Index